WOMEN IN MULTIFAMILY REAL ESTATE

How Queens Do Apartment Investing Differently

KAYLEE MCMAHON

Women in Multifamily Real Estate
ISBN: 978-1-946694-48-5

Library of Congress Control Number: 2021906611

TABLE OF CONTENTS

DEDICATION

To my sisters...

Learning from my mess, the best advice I can give you is to ask for what you want... for the dream relationship, job, health, spirituality, wealth, adventures, and anything else. You CAN have them all when you learn to ask for help. You MUST ask for help to have the life you deserve.

Practice stoicism in everything. You cannot control the thoughts, actions, perceptions, or words of others. But you sure as hell can control yours! Doing this has given me inner peace.

We must become self-aware of our traumas, habits, and co-dependencies. Ask yourself if the things you repeat every day, including drinking coffee, help you achieve your end goal faster?

We must become truly wise and realize we have NONE of the answers. Strive to always learn from the wise.

My success is due entirely to the behavior described above.

Once you do the inner work, having success in multifamily will flow. Anything will flow, for that matter.

Let's become empowered through self-trust and self-belief to become financially empowered!

Initial Thoughts

I've met so many women in this business who freely share their knowledge and experience. This book is the result of conversations with successful women in multifamily real estate investing who have touched my life and the lives of countless others. These women are resilient, wise, professional, and want to help others get ahead by sharing defining moments and lessons learned in their journey to success.

I wrote this book to give interested investors a snapshot of WHO it takes to win in multifamily investing. My message is 1000% about finding the right people who are in alignment with your journey.

I'm grateful to the women who were willing to tell their stories. I learned so much from each of them during our conversations, and I'm sure you will find value in the knowledge they impart.

They are true mentors and educators, and exactly the kind of people you want on your team.

When building your team, ensure you have:

1. A deal finder who fronts risk/partial risk capital

2. Excellence in operations (asset manager)

3. Baller money raiser/investor relations

4. Vetted vendors (we have used them before, and they all are high performing)

5. Key principles and partners with enough deal experience to obtain a non-recourse agency loan if needed

All team members work together to complete tasks and get the deal across the finish line. Then, post-closing, each has a lane and respectfully stays in it.

My journey into real estate investing started from my need to escape abuse. Cash-flowing real estate was my way out, and I am no longer a victim. Did you know that one-third of women are abused, and 98% of domestic violence victims also experience financial abuse, which causes longer-lasting damage?

Abuse = Power = Financial Power Over Women

What can we do about it?

1. Reduce poverty and empower women by giving them access to life-changing passive income from apartment investing.

2. Through technology, provide investment and financial education to remove the fear of money.

Solving this problem is at the heart of The Apartment Queen, as shown in our Mission, Vision, Values and Beliefs.

MISSION

The Apartment Queen's mission is to stop abuse and codependent relationships by providing women with investment opportunities and making education about creating wealth through real estate investing readily available. This creates the mindset for financial and other freedoms, ultimately leading individuals to find and live their why and purpose in life.

The above mission statement isn't just words — this is how I live my life every day. Everything I do requires a time investment to ensure I have a purpose and that my partners share the same mission and alignment.

VISION

We WILL change the world, create financial independence for one billion women investors, and create one billion "givers" by 2030.

CORE BELIEFS AND VALUES

Teammates make decisions with open, constructive communication.

We make strong, good, and positive statements while focusing on building our strengths.

Emotions are good at the right time and place.

We are grateful for everyone and everything we have.

We believe that ethics are key.

We want to help steer others in the right direction when we don't have the answer.

We're always honest with RADICAL TRANSPARENCY and OPEN-MINDEDNESS.

We keep our word while under-promising and over-delivering results.

Compliments are constant.

We treat others how we want to be treated.

We stand up to bullies.

We put families first.

We focus on running a business using principles.

We always ask questions and never assume.

We always ask for help-shit happens.

Mental and physical health is a priority.

We celebrate all wins.

We want to know and nurture each employee's Personal financial and business goals.

We want employees to regularly share good news, what they love/loathe in their role, where they are stuck, new ideas, fears, concerns, decisions, opportunities, and feedback from customers/employees.

If you are 1000% on-board with the above, this team is for you. This belief will show itself in actions. Over time, people I meet who think these are cool words eventually fade off, and that is OK. I want to be up-front and clear. No surprises.

I'm always learning, and I hope this book inspires you to take the time to educate yourself about real estate investing. Remember, you are not in it alone.

I truly hope you enjoy this book. It was written with you in mind.

WOMEN IN MULTIFAMILY REAL ESTATE

KAYLEE MCMAHON

Featuring:

Sara Laschever

Kelly Stinson

Kim Stallings, MBA

Lisa Hylton

Karolina DiMario

Kathy Fettke

Shannon Shackerley-Bennett

Dawn Waye

Karen Oeser

Leka Devatha

Lizzy Neutz

Brooke Jackson

Pili Yarusi

Erin Hudson

Cindy Mirliss

Ann Cone

Anna Kelley

Amy Tiemann

Kristy Siple

Chat Steinwald

Sandhya Seshadri

The Apartment
Queen

We are looking for more investors like you.

Please complete The Apartment Queen™
Investor Questionnaire to be added to
our list for events and deals:
https://form.jotform.com/200207883604451

Our ideal investor is typically one of these following
Ultimate passive investors:
WOMEN with 1031 Exchange over $400K
High Net Worth Individuals
Doctors
Dentists
Engineers
Individual with 10 Years' Experience at a Company
Real Estate Brokers/Agents
Female Athletes
Aggie Women
Women CEO, Founder
Socialites
Duchess/Heiress
Individuals with Pension Funds
Endowments
Women-owned Family Offices
Those with Funds Who Support the Social Initiative
to Teach Financial Literacy to Women
Angel Investors Supporting Women

Chapter 1 – Advantages for Females in Real Estate Investing

More than half of *real estate agents* are female, so you might assume that women are well-represented in the real estate industry. Unfortunately, it's not the case because only thirty percent of *real estate investors* are women. But that figure will soon increase as more women discover the built-in benefits of flipping and fixing properties to generate profits.

Women Who Flip

Although there are some famous female property flippers on HGTV, many people still think you should leave real estate construction to men. It is not surprising that networks like HGTV choose prominent female REI-flippers because they firmly believe in their passion.

Dallas, Texas is still a hot market for flipping. Veteran investors are snagging properties near metro stops, famous with millennials, including older row houses to convert to multifamily units.

A savvy flipper can purchase a single row house for $500,000, remodel, and sell each unit from $650,000 to $950,000. So, why do females still comprise a small piece of the pie, and what are the routes they can take to success?

Becoming a Real Estate Investor

Many real estate investors begin as home inspectors, wholesalers, appraisers, or contractors—all of which tend to be dominated by men. But there are other paths to becoming a real estate investor. Realtors are excellent candidates for real estate investors because they have a thorough knowledge of local markets, pricing, and sales cycles.

So what does it take to become an influential female real estate investor? Confidence and knowledge are crucial—understand the market and the figures needed to translate it to a profit. Successful real estate investors should not guess or rely on intuition when buying properties. Instead, develop a system for analyzing properties based on the numbers.

Persistence is essential, and investors should follow up on every lead. Create relationships with resources such as hard money lenders and real estate agents. Also, find a mentor or veteran investor who is willing to answer newbie questions.

THE EDGE OF FEMALE REAL ESTATE INVESTORS

Women naturally excel at the skills needed for real estate investing, such as creating relationships, networking, and problem-solving. Additionally, women often have family support or a working spouse who has a steady income.

Being a woman in real estate investing has many more advantages than disadvantages. So, what are you waiting for?

Chapter 2 – Attracting Women to Real Estate Investing

Most women feel confident handling daily financial responsibilities like balancing a checkbook and maintaining a household budget. Women are the primary decision-makers when purchasing property or vehicles.

But few women move beyond a personal purchase and invest in real estate. They maintain their money in checking or savings accounts instead of investing those funds because they lack confidence and knowledge. Only about 30 percent of real estate investors are women.

Listed below are some ways of guiding women to engage in real estate investing and breaking this trend.

Encourage Confidence. Studies show that women lack confidence in the realm of investing. To increase confidence, learn the trades in residential and commercial real estate investment and emulate the demeanor of other real estate professionals. Unravel the possibilities and the real-world profits investors in real estate are seeing.

Connect with Other Investors to Find the Best Deals. When searching for the perfect investment, join local investment clubs, attend meetings at your local Chamber of Commerce, Rotary Clubs, and economic development councils, and reach out to local real estate agencies.

Find a Coach or Mentor. Look for a real estate agent or investor who is successful in your market. Ensure it is someone who has an in-depth analysis of the market and understands its fluctuations. Working with someone equipped with the right amount of experience whom you can depend on to help you make the best decision on a property is ideal.

Know the Language. Listen to the podcasts and read popular real estate news from sources like RealTrends, Inman, and Realtor Magazine, and become familiar with common terms.

Start Small But Think Big. Incorporating one rental property within your portfolio every few years can help you build your retirement and reach your financial goals.

Chapter 3 – Common Communication Traps for Women in Business

Good communication is essential for any successful business, including internal (with employees, co-workers, and team members) and external (clients, lenders, contractors).

Lack of or poor communication can lead to misunderstandings, confusion, and conflicts. However, effective communication skills can set you apart from your competitors.

Below are some communication traps women commonly fall into:

1– Over-Apologizing

Sorry, not sorry.

Women apologize more often than men. Men only apologize when they BELIEVE they have done something wrong. Women do it as a knee-jerk reaction to show empathy or when they believe they are wrong, such as:

- When scooting in chairs

- As a conversation filler

- When passing others or getting in their way if they are looking at something

- When they are unable to schedule something at a specific time

Apologizing like this undermines power and effectiveness. So, how can this be fixed?

- Encourage men to apologize more

- Encourage women to apologize less

- Accept the imbalance

WHAT DO APOLOGIES DO?

Apologies cause damage. Repeated apologies lose their meaning like the boy who cried wolf. The more often you do it, the more it damages the sincerity of a genuine apology. Also, it creates the perception of wrongdoing even if you didn't do anything wrong, impacting the balance of power. When you continually ask for forgiveness, you essentially allow someone else to choose if you should be forgiven. You can, of course, forgive yourself for little things.

In business, where we must demand respect to progress in our careers, it's important to apologize and admit true mistakes, but not over-apologize. Doing this shows we are responsible and mature enough to fix problems we create and establishes trust when we really make a mistake.

Think about your habits. When do you apologize? Is it mainly knee-jerk reactions? Do you often apologize to someone you see as a superior? Are you filling time? Are you apologizing for someone else's mistake or something you did?

THREE STEPS TO FORMING A PROPER APOLOGY

1. Express Regret

2. Take Responsibility

3. Provide a Remedy

Never make excuses or point the finger at someone else. You want to be able to say, "I do not and have never blamed x mistake on anyone else but me. I own it." This clearly states that you aren't and won't attempt to lessen the authenticity of your apology.

2 – OVER-SHARING

Women tend to over-share, believing this creates empathy or understanding. In the workplace, unfortunately, there is a line between sharing/ being professional and over-sharing. It is important to have a good rapport. For example, when a co-worker asks how your child's birthday party went, you can answer honestly, "It was a disaster." Leave it at that, and don't detail how your in-laws brought up an old skeleton, starting an argument that ruined the birthday party and caused you to drink a bottle of wine.

Even if we are not judgmental, we are subject to someone's general perception. We must remember that most people operate by judgments and perception. We cannot control that; we can only control our actions and our perceptions of others.

Save personal details for those who are in your personal life. Fight the impulse to share things with others because you believe doing so could build a strong bond. Avoid the possibility that a co-worker or peer would interpret you sharing personal details to mean you want to be more than friends.

Also, keep in mind that the more you reveal about yourself, the more opportunities you create for opportunistic people to get in. Be wary of those you allow in your organization.

Unintended Consequences of Over-Sharing

- Wastes time

- Erodes respect (sounds crazy, but it's how some people are)

- Creates a false sense of intimacy with the listener

When it comes to reports, list only the facts. Do not include others' shortcomings or a heroic story of what you did. Leave openings for plenty of questions.

3 – Increase Your Worth with Your Words

A large percentage of women point out their physical and other inadequacies, which, at a minimum, increases cortisol levels. But this can also impact your worth. For example, if someone asks where you work, instead of replying, "I work at a lab," say, "I work at a lab where we are researching the cure for brain cancer. What you do?"

"I work in IT" would be another example. Consider saying, "I work at a security company that keeps healthcare records safe from cyber-criminals" instead. Do you need help figuring out what your super-powers are?

Answer these questions:

- What do you love to do?

- What do others regularly thank you for doing?

- What are you great at doing?

Once you can form a reply that addresses each of these questions, you can define why you are both super and powerful.

CHAPTER 4 – EMOTIONS AND WOMEN IN MULTIFAMILY REAL ESTATE

Multifamily real estate is much like a game of chess. To win, you can't allow your opponents or employees to know how you are feeling. It is essential to not react in a way that would upset the team or make them feel unsure, such as hurt, anger, and fear. You can always display approval, excitement, joy, gratitude, and even personal sadness (family issues). But when it comes to apartment challenges and how they make you feel, you must have the strength to deal with your feelings on your own time.

WOMEN DEAL WITH CHALLENGES DIFFERENTLY

Women and men behave very differently when dealing with issues or challenges that affect them, alienating and discouraging those around them. Men learn to be tough and not to let their feelings show. Women often wear their hearts on their sleeves. Men have feelings, too, but men and women deal with and display our feelings in very different ways.

As a woman, I've learned that I cannot sweep the hard feelings under the rug. For me, seeing a therapist, journaling, blogging, meditating, and focusing on calm deep breathing is key, especially when I notice that I am affected by others' reactions. It's important to remain professional and level-headed at all times.

When I don't know the answer to a problem, I tell others that I need a couple of days to think through the challenge at hand. My team must understand that they can always turn to me as a resource. When I'm struggling to find the path forward, I reach out to my mentors for their insight on the best decision.

ASK FOR HELP

I surround myself with professionals and mentors who serve as a council or board of sorts. I aim to share my feelings and challenges with them, openly and honestly. This is important for both women and men because mentors understand what you're going through and can offer advice from their experiences.

One of the biggest lessons in multifamily real estate is that it does not happen successfully without teamwork. Your team includes those you lean on for guidance and empowerment, even if they are not financially involved in the deal.

As a single, hard-working female who has been alone for many years pursuing a career and purpose in life, I often have difficulty accepting help from others. Part of me feels inadequate for not knowing all the answers, but I take comfort knowing that none of us have all the answers (even those with 20 or 30 years of experience in the industry). So, I push myself to ask for help when I need it, rather than living on an island.

Dealing with conflict is often a part of our upbringing. In some households, women are more emotional. Growing up in my house, it was the exact opposite. Some people mistake my ability to separate feelings from what must be done as a masculine trait. I am merely behaving as I remember the women around me behaving throughout my life, which has helped me do well in multifamily during moments of uncertainty, stress, doubt, and others attempting to play on my subconscious insecurities as a woman.

TAKE CARE OF YOURSELF

Self-love and self-confidence are vital to anyone involved in multifamily real estate. Your actions affect thousands of people, their homes, and entire communities. Whether you are a woman or a man, putting in the work to truly understand and love yourself and move forward knowing these things is critical. Some women avoid multifamily real estate because they worry about balancing raising children while working in a high-stress industry. Should I choose to have children, I have complete confidence that I can delegate tasks to the correct people and succeed in anything I choose, with the right support, of course.

Remember, when anyone tells you something that "should" hold you back or challenges your strengths, that is 100% "their shit," and you shouldn't take on their self-doubt and problems.

WOMEN CAN WIN BIG IN MULTIFAMILY REAL ESTATE

Women have an incredible intuitive ability to make decisions. When we love ourselves and listen to and believe ourselves, we tend to be better investors, early adopters, and overall less risky decision-makers.

When women take the time to believe in their knowledge, decisions, and self-worth, we can be a significant asset to any team.

COMMUNICATE YOUR WANTS AND NEEDS – NO ONE IS A MIND READER

Nothing breaks up partnerships faster than failure to communicate. Women tend to internalize what they want instead of expressing it out loud or negotiating. A good negotiator:

- Is secure in asking for what they want

- Asks for more than they think they can get

- Understands both parties need to eat

- Knows everything we do is a negotiation

If we don't negotiate, resentment builds. Speak up because no one can read your mind.

Accepting that you will need to put in the extra effort to express your wants and needs to your partners is absolutely critical. Of course, it's important to proceed professionally, putting any negative or hurt feelings aside, dealing with your feelings on your own time, and negotiating to where you want to be.

YOU ARE RUNNING A BUSINESS

Remember, you are running a business. Although apartments are "housing," owning an apartment complex is not the same as flipping a house, developing a subdivision, or other types of real estate investing.

By operating as a business owner, women have a leg up on men because of our intuition. We make less risky investments and project success for the long-haul.

Cheers to all the Women in Multifamily Real Estate! I can't wait to see more women playing in this arena with me.

Chapter 5 – Don't Be a Bitch

Introduction

This chapter is probably my favorite in this book. I am curious if the meaning is still applicable because the word "bitch" usually implies a derogatory notion, such as when used by a man to describe another man. He says, "Don't be a little bit...". Or when someone refers to an assertive woman or boss, they will say, "One hell of a bit..." or other similar expressions.

Many of us have been targets of this term, whose meaning has evolved over the years. We'll unravel its true meaning from my experience in the multifamily real estate industry. Once we understand the traditional definition of a "bitch," it's time to identify how NOT to behave and instead be a "bad ass bitch" and take that word back.

Who is a Bitch?

In multifamily real estate, a bitch is someone you are dealing with who wants to hurt you instead of helping you. It's essential that you recognize this character trait, which is prevalent in business. Otherwise, you may find yourself worse off than before you met them.

Be wary of anyone who always tries to pressure you or make you believe things that you know are not true or accurate. Stay away from those who criticize your strengths.

Let me give you an example. Everybody knows that I am a wiz at social media, and I am everywhere within the online realm. I am very comfortable in my skin, and I really like myself. Through the years, I have defined my self-confidence and how I handle myself. After years of struggling with my self-image, beliefs, and purpose in life, I have built up my character. It took many years to get me to the place I am now.

Once you establish yourself and an educator and advocate, you can host a podcast or post on social media to share information. Although there is no charge for others to access this information, it is valuable and will allow others to succeed.

It may be difficult at first, but you should ignore any negative comments on your posts. Don't allow others to make you doubt your expertise and prevent you from doing what you enjoy. Some people have nothing better to do than manipulate you and rain on your parade, commonly referred to as "bullies." Women in the multifamily real estate industry look out for one another and will not tolerate this negative behavior.

As part of our core values, we do not accept bullying. Anyone who tries to bully my people or me, attempts to infiltrate my life negatively, or makes derogatory comments about another's strengths has no place in my life or my company. Stay away from people who do such things.

When relationships are severed In the multifamily real estate industry, everyone knows about it and wants to understand what happened. If a passive investor or an active general partner in a deal treats others maliciously, wants to control everyone, and has a hidden agenda, no one in this industry will want to do business with them.

It is very important that you know you do not belong in the multifamily industry if you feel the need to control other people. You are better off working on your own simply because there is no reason to do that to anyone. That is weakness, not leadership.

No one should be able to control somebody else's thoughts and feelings as well as perceptions. Neither should you control somebody's actions. However, you have the power and right to control your actions, perception, and, of course, your words. And our mantra should be, "Do not choose or accept or let anybody in our life, who is a bully."

THE ONE WHERE SOMEBODY PUTS OTHERS DOWN

Bullies are often narcissists and will put others down to make themselves feel good, take control, and expose others' weaknesses to their advantage. They are only out for themselves and enjoy controlling others for the sole purpose of feeding their ego. I have lived through this, and it will drain everything you have. IF you see a partner, vendor, or anyone treating others like this, you better believe the same shit is happening to you. Do not ignore this behavior.

Some women in business believe they must be autocratic and think like a man. They think that they should be dominant in their place of business. An autocratic person leads by force, ensuring everyone knows he/she is the boss, they are in charge, and everyone should answer to him/her. Women are naturally democratic and not autocratic. Those women who behave like men often feel like they have to compensate for something they are not. They feel the need to prove their sameness and be accepted by men while reducing the power and strength of others. This weakens a woman's power to collaborate and give everyone's unique skills a seat at the table. Collaborative groups are a force to be reckoned with.

There is simply no reason why any female would need to be an autocratic leader. Successful female leaders are collaborative and democratic at the same time. We work well in teams and focus on our strengths instead of highlighting our weaknesses.

LACK OF CONTROL

In my early 20s, I was a pretty laid-back person, but I tended to control simple things like cleaning the house and feeding the dogs. Perhaps I worried about my appearance and my shortcomings, causing me to want to control people or things outside my realm, which was a big mistake. A Bitch controls other people. Don't be a bitch.

Women in multifamily real estate investing should understand that they will not be able to control everything. Something will go wrong no matter how prepared you are. Accept that and know that you are capable of handling anything that comes your way. Fretting about it trying to ensure everything is perfect is a complete waste of time and energy. Focus on what you can control

ARE YOU LITIGIOUS?

Someone who is litigious is not a good fit for the multifamily real estate industry. *Litigious* is a negative term, which describes a negative action. Nobody says that they are litigious, but when their actions do not complement what they say, well…people SHOW US who they are. When somebody attacks you with multiple lawsuits and says they are not litigious, it is a total load of shit. Stand your ground. Work within your mission and vision and exude your core values when working with others. One of mine includes "abuse, in any form, is unacceptable."

Avoid evil behaviors.

Our Mission, Vision, and Values

Our mission is to avoid abuse and toxic co-dependent relationships by providing investment opportunities and digital education for women to acquire wealth through real estate investing. Generating a financial mindset will lead individuals to discover and unravel their purpose in life.

Our "Vision 2030" is to change the world by achieving financial literacy and independence for one billion women all over the globe.

Further, our core beliefs and values ensure that teammates make decisions with open, constructive communication—a principle of meritocracy where the idea with the most merit wins. You should conduct negotiations and make business decisions without emotions.

We always make it a point to be grateful for everyone and everything we have. We always focus on what we have, not what we don't have. No matter how it sounds, we always tell the truth. We practice transparency, and always have an open mind. Integrity is a must. Our business operates with gratefulness, appreciation, transparency, and integrity. We have zero tolerance for bullying.

Mental health is as important as physical health. We always ask questions and never make assumptions. Celebrating triumphs, big or small, and rewarding those who do a great job is essential.

We embody our mission, vision, and values while avoiding those who are not in line with how we operate.

Anyone operating a multifamily real estate business should be mindful of the parameters listed above. Bullies, narcissists, manipulative, controlling, litigious, only for yourself, and autocratic individuals will not do well in this industry. Women with those characteristics are who I label with the traditional b-word meaning and are not reasonable, let alone a good team player. A lot of money is at stake in a multifamily investment, and frivolous lawsuits serve little purpose. Behaving like a bitch is unacceptable.

It is essential to lean on your team and work with your team.

Finally, all I can say is, let's team up like the "bad bitches" we are. Put each other first, and use our conservative, collaborative, and team-player natural skills to be the best multifamily investment firm there ever was. Together you will go far.

The Apartment Queen

We are looking for more investors like you.

**Please complete The Apartment Queen™
Investor Questionnaire to be added to
our list for events and deals:**
https://form.jotform.com/200207883604451

Our ideal investor is typically one of these following
Ultimate passive investors:
WOMEN with 1031 Exchange over $400K
High Net Worth Individuals
Doctors
Dentists
Engineers
Individual with 10 Years' Experience at a Company
Real Estate Brokers/Agents
Female Athletes
Aggie Women
Women CEO, Founder
Socialites
Duchess/Heiress
Individuals with Pension Funds
Endowments
Women-owned Family Offices
Those with Funds Who Support the Social Initiative
to Teach Financial Literacy to Women
Angel Investors Supporting Women

Chapter 6 – Actions Speak Louder Than Your Chest

Women in any industry, not just multifamily real estate, should understand the many facets of doing business with men. In 2021, less than 30% of the Commercial Real estate industry is female. Some wonder if women use their feminine ways to get what they want in a male-dominated field? Or in other words, "Do women have to flirt to win business?"

It is very easy to do; however, flirting to get a deal WILL bite you in the butt or undermine your true capabilities and what you can offer EVERY TIME. To make an impact in business, you must have credibility. Your actions should reflect who you are and how you behave. Remember, "Actions speak louder than words," or in this case, "Actions speak louder than your chest."

Closing the Deal

Should women use their femininity or persuasive power to get a better deal in business? Well, at the right time and in the right way, you can use it to close a deal or during negotiation.

Let me clarify. You can never properly negotiate or close a deal without mutual respect from each party. The business relationship should be long-term, so ensure that it is a win/win.

Women do not want to use sex appeal to get ahead in business. Still, it often seems our male counterparts push that narrative, causing many women to wonder if it is a normal, acceptable way to do business.

This fear often discourages women from entering typically male-dominated industries such as technology, engineering, and commercial real estate. Negative thoughts and self-limiting beliefs often hold women back from doing what they need. In a group where you are the minority, this creates self-believed limitations or stereotypes such as thinking, "I'm bad at math," even if you're not.

USE YOUR SKILLS

Women should never feel like they need to use their looks to get ahead because they have many other valuable skills. For example, women are typically better listeners than men. In conversations, people will share more information when they see the other party is attentive and listening. This can uncover weaknesses or information that you need for a stronger position in a later deal—everything is a negotiation.

#1 ADVICE TO WIN AS A FEMALE IN BUSINESS EVERY TIME

I have witnessed time and again that women want to discuss personal relationships. We will voluntarily open up about spouses, kids, or dating escapades. You should listen intently if the male across the table from you is saying these things about himself. Try to ask engaging questions that relate to their story so that you keep them on their train of thought. Ask more open-ended questions, "Oh, and how many children did you say you have?" Keep them talking about their relationships because there might be key information they plan to share with you.

DO NOT interrupt or try to establish similarities with your relationships; that's the key to success. And this is not rocket science—this principle has been handed down from female entrepreneurs to other female entrepreneurs. I REPEAT…DO NOT share anything about your personal relationships. Not your spouse, kids, dating, or romantic interests. Nothing like this! Don't let his mind wander and envision you as more than a professional. He should stare at you and scratch his head thinking, "I don't know if she's married, has kids or what." Keep him guessing. It's fine to discuss grandma dying, an issue with a sibling, etc.; you are human, after all. But leave personal relationships out of the conversation. When I mention my boyfriend, I refer to him as a "very close friend," which enables me to discuss only topics related to making money and business, which does not apply to romance.

BOUNDARIES

Navigate the conversation carefully to avoid coming across as defensive to your male counterparts. It is acceptable to talk about your personal life, but you need to have defined boundaries for relationships. Human beings are inherently curious, and not everyone has the discipline to control their curiosity or their perceptions.

Some may not be at the point of maturity or growth to control their thoughts and actions. Others choose not to control those things, so you have to be SMARTER and steer the conversation for them if you want to be on top of the deal.

For example, if the other party's broker is talking about their spouse, allow them to continue to speak. Let the conversation flow, but if you are asked about your relationship status, quickly change the topic with a smile—that is the secret. It definitely helps if you are engaged in a face-to-face meeting or even a Zoom meeting. The important thing is that you see the person to whom you are speaking.

If the other person does not seem to acknowledge your subtle attempts to change the subject, pause for a second and let the silence settle. The other party will read your body language and realize this subject crosses a boundary.

Unfortunately, some people are clueless, and it is not attributable to gender. After the pause, slowly state with a smile, "I would like to ask you what you need in your role to be successful and how I can help you." Answering a question about relationships is not necessary. YOU DO NOT OWE ANYONE AN ANSWER OR EXPLANATION. Keep your power.

Make sure your pause results in a positive interaction but definitively expresses that you are not interested in discussing personal relationships. If they bring the topic up again, take another more aggressive pause and shift the conversation to business.

If it continues, ask yourself, "Do I want to do business with that person?" They do not respect boundaries, which everyone requires to be successful and to trust others. So, that may be your "sign" or "red flag" that this negotiation/deal/partnership should probably not happen. It's not worth pursuing a working relationship with that person.

OTHER RED FLAGS

Anything that requires time and effort will surely take money away from you. Instead of wasting time on unproductive meetings that make you feel uncomfortable, do not dwell on them. There are other opportunities, money, and deals out there. Secure your credibility, reputation, sanity, and, more importantly, your composure—nobody else will do it for you. This is true self-care.

These lessons are not new but can be easy to forget. When you live by these principles, there is an excellent possibility that you will meet success. When you give value to others, regardless of gender, you radiate something in the universe. Others will see you as a professional.

Remember, when you put the right things out there, that's what will present itself in your life.

MULTIFAMILY INVESTING BASICS

Chapter 7 – Benefits of Investing in Multifamily Properties

Investing in multifamily properties is an excellent way for investors to diversify their real estate portfolios.

Multifamily Property

Any property that contains two or more units within the same building is considered a multifamily property. Each unit has a living room, bathroom, and kitchen, although the size and shape of each may vary.

Some common examples of multifamily properties include duplexes, townhomes, and apartment complexes.

Investing in Multifamily Properties

Many families and individuals at various stages in their lives view multifamily housing as the best and most affordable option. The high demand for multifamily properties results in a lower vacancy rate, making them preferred among real estate investors.

Some benefits to investing in multifamily properties include:

Increased Cash Flow

Unlike single-family homes where you receive one payment, multifamily investing generates greater cash flow and minimizes investor risk because several tenants pay rent each month.

Lower Acquisition Cost Per Unit

On a per-unit basis, multifamily property construction is more affordable than other types of real estate properties. If you choose to apply for a mortgage loan to build or purchase a multifamily property, you may find lower financing rates than single-family homes.

Lower Foreclosure Rates

The foreclosure rate for multifamily properties is lower than a single-family home, which explains why mortgage lenders can offer more competitive rates for investors in this type of property. Reduced operating costs will increase revenue.

Easier to Manage

Managing ten units under one roof is easier than managing ten individual rental properties spread all over the city. Generally, this type of investment justifies hiring a property manager who can help to optimize the investment.

Tax Breaks

Local governments provide tax incentives to multifamily property investors for providing housing in their city. The incentives vary depending on the property classification. Tax breaks result in added revenues.

High Appreciation Rate

The value for multifamily properties typically increases faster than other property types (although this is not guaranteed).

A well-maintained property with curb appeal will attract more potential renters, increase rental amounts, and add to the property's value.

Less Investment Risk

All investments carry some risk. The risks for investing in multifamily properties are considerably lower than investing in other property types, including single-family homes.

The primary risk is a high vacancy rate, but since you have multiple tenants, the risk of having a completely vacant property is relatively low.

Build Your Investment Portfolio Faster

Multifamily investing can boost a serious investor's portfolio quickly. If you want to invest in multiple units, a multifamily property is an excellent option. It is easier to acquire one property with multiple units than several single-family homes.

SUMMARY

Every type of real estate investment carries its own set of risks and benefits. If you are serious about investing in multifamily properties, ensure that you study the market and the specific location.

Be aware of any risks so you can avoid them. Like with stocks, you can employ several strategies to mitigate any risks associated with your investment. Proper due diligence can help protect you from any significant losses.

We are looking for more investors like you.

**Please complete The Apartment Queen™
Investor Questionnaire to be added to
our list for events and deals:**
https://form.jotform.com/200207883604451

Our ideal investor is typically one of these following
Ultimate passive investors:
WOMEN with 1031 Exchange over $400K
High Net Worth Individuals
Doctors
Dentists
Engineers
Individual with 10 Years' Experience at a Company
Real Estate Brokers/Agents
Female Athletes
Aggie Women
Women CEO, Founder
Socialites
Duchess/Heiress
Individuals with Pension Funds
Endowments
Women-owned Family Offices
Those with Funds Who Support the Social Initiative
to Teach Financial Literacy to Women
Angel Investors Supporting Women

Chapter 8 – Apartment Syndication Explained

A syndicate in real estate is a group of investors who combine their resources (capital, time, and knowledge) to increase their buying power to purchase a property.

The practice of teaming up to purchase real started hundreds of years ago. Real estate entrepreneurs or professionals (now known as "sponsors") could advertise their investment ideas to anyone. Today, this is referred to as "public solicitation." The Securities Act of 1933 required all new securities offerings to be registered with the Securities Exchange Commission (SEC) to provide oversight and protect investors from fraud.

As a result, registering each offering and jumping through the necessary hoops made syndication less efficient, effectively ending public solicitation. Syndicators were forced to gather capital from a private "black book" of money sources, including fellow country club members, family trusts, working professionals, etc. Real estate syndications were quietly put together and relied heavily on personal connections or licensed fund brokers.

Private syndication continues today and is what we do at The Apartment Queen. We can issue securities as long as:

1. No more than 35 sophisticated investors participate in the 506(b) offering

2. Each investor completes an Investor Questionnaire/Self Certifies

3. Accredited investors obtain third-party verification that they qualify as Accredited Investors in a 506(c) offering

Parties in an Apartment Syndication

A sponsor has the knowledge and experience to locate, analyze, and purchase a multifamily property with major upside (investment earnings potential).

Passive investors (from here on referred to as equity partners) usually don't have the experience, free time, and funds to purchase commercial multifamily property on their own.

When you buy a property in a syndication model, you are part of a group of investors who all own shares of the property. The syndicator may allow the sale of shares in some specific cases, such as when an investor becomes ill or experiences a hardship. You may be able to sell your shares to other investors inside or outside of the group.

Equity partners often have the misconception that their money will be inaccessible during the entire hold period (the time that the property is held under ownership by all members/shareholders in the LLC) when investing in a syndication. Hold periods typically average five to seven years (The Apartment Queen hold times range from 3-5 years).

Before investing as an equity partner, do your due diligence and learn if the prospective syndicator will allow investors to sell their shares, how, to whom, and under what circumstances.

PRIVATE PLACEMENT MEMORANDUM (PPM)

When investing in a syndication, you will be required to sign a PPM —a SUPER LENGTHY legal document required by the SEC and written by our knowledgeable securities attorney. The PPM includes the partnership agreement, outlines all the information about the project, lists the method of compensation, fee structures, preferred returns (if stated), business plan, and details on how income and appreciation will be distributed. It also addresses under which circumstances an investor can replace themselves as equity partners.

The PPM will be your "go to" document for everything about the syndication deal. Many investors don't read these, but please try. It contains a treasure trove of information, such as:

Intro paragraph – provides a summary of the deal.

"Risk Factors" section – The down and dirty of the deal and where you want to spend most of your time. No one knows the risks more than the sponsor who put the deal together. Our experienced SEC attorney writes this section for all of our deals because if there were ever a lawsuit, we could show the sponsor did their job to explain the risks.

Syndicates are commonly structured as Limited Liability Companies (LLCs). This special-purpose entity is the preferred method for investors to purchase property, like apartment complexes we purchase at The Apartment Queen.

IMPORTANT QUESTIONS INVESTORS SHOULD ASK

- What are the loan terms?
- What type of loan did the sponsor get?
- What is the interest rate?
- How long is the interest rate fixed?
- How much money was put down?
- Is the philosophy to pay down debt and then distribute the money? Or is there a return that can change after five years?
- Is there an interest-only loan?

HOW IS THE SYNDICATION FUNDED? HOW MUCH DO YOU NEED TO CLOSE?

Sponsors typically must come up with the remaining cash to close after the loan coverage (75/25 loan-to-value is common, leaving the sponsor to raise 25% of the money for acquisition and development) plus additional soft costs/closing costs.

The Apartment Queen relies on private individuals to raise this money. This benefits equity partners greatly and offers to opportunity to make life-changing income.

For example, on our last project, a 50K capital contribution (excluding quarterly payouts) ended up turning into 105% of that on sale. We also offer equity partners the chance to own 70-75% of the asset, even though managers do all the work. To do this, we must have access to other investors who can help fund our deals. Otherwise, we have to use debt lenders who provide all the capital for 50% of the deal, and none of my friends or family benefit from the hard work that we do. I LOVE making my friends RICH.

WHAT ABOUT THE STOCK MARKET?

Investing in the stock market is much different than investing in multifamily properties. Real estate investments carry many benefits, such as depreciation and expense write-off. The stock market is highly volatile, changing from one day to the next.

WORKING WITH SOMEONE "NEW" TO THE SYNDICATION GAME

Investing with an early operator who is just starting can be a slam dunk investment. Newer operators are eager to make you happy, provide overly favorable terms, and in many cases, are willing to take a loss on you so that they can get your business again and referrals! Searching out a new player with the above due diligence can be a superior combination.

THE APARTMENT QUEEN RETURNS

We payout quarterly cash on cash after the first year value-add period.

If the project is a heavy value play, we will usually (not always) refinance and distribute cash to shareholders.

On sale, we will distribute additional checks. This is the big one.

So, you could possibly make three returns: cash on cash, refinance cash out, and sale returns.

We have seen 9% cash on cash and 85-100% return on sale for our past projects (this past performance in no way guarantees or influences future returns).

INVESTING IN MULTIFAMILY

If you're interested in more information about upcoming multifamily investment projects and how we can serve you, email us at admin@theapartmentqueen.com.

Or

Take our investor quiz so we can let you know about future events and deals. Find "The Apartment Queen™ Investor Questionnaire" at: https://form.jotform.com/200207883604451

CHAPTER 9 – ACCREDITED AND SOPHISTICATED INVESTORS

The Securities and Exchanges Commission (SEC) protects investors by restricting who can put their money into high-risk, loosely regulated, or complex financial offerings. The SEC encourages or requires companies that are raising capital through private offerings to work with accredited investors. However, the rules allow a certain number of non-accredited investors to participate if they meet specific disclosure requirements.

ACCREDITED INVESTORS

The SEC defines an *Accredited Investor* as someone who is assumed to have the financial expertise to handle complex and potentially risky investment transactions. An accreditor investor can invest in securities, such as a multifamily syndication, by satisfying the net worth requirements listed below:

1. Earned annual income of $200,000 for individuals or $300,000 for couples filing jointly for the previous two years and reasonably expects the same for the current year.

OR

2. Has a net worth of over $1 million, either alone or with a spouse (excluding the value of the primary residence).

The SEC created this definition to:

- Identity investors and entities who are considered "sophisticated" and can absorb a potential financial loss.

- Protect inexperienced investors from getting into riskier projects, especially if they do not have the financial means to cover a loss.

- Regulate investment companies against advertising to or soliciting investments from non-accredited investors.

ACCREDITATION ADVANTAGES

Being an accredited investor enables you to learn about more deals, gain access to them, and ultimately invest. Accredited investor opportunities include:

- Real Estate Syndications (Private Placements)
- Angel Investing/Venture Capital
- Hedge Funds

BECOMING AN ACCREDITED INVESTOR

Anyone can claim accredited investor status by:

- Checking a box on a legal document certifying they are an accredited investor
- Indicating the method by which they meet the qualification requirements
- Confirming they understand the implications involved

Some types of private placement offerings may require investors to submit a letter of verification from a CPA, attorney, broker-dealer, or third-party verification service.

Investors should only certify that they are accredited investors if they truly are. Falsely claiming accreditation could result in legal ramifications for the investor and the company with whom they invest.

SOPHISTICATED INVESTORS

If you issue an offering under Rule 506 (b), investment dollars can be accepted from non-accredited investors if they are *Sophisticated Investors*. (This is the *only* exception to the accreditation rule.)

The SEC defines a sophisticated investor as an individual or institution that "must have sufficient knowledge and experience in financial and business matters to make them capable of evaluating the merits and risks of the prospective investment."

This loosely-defined term in the financial and legal worlds describes individuals or institutions with significant market experience, knowledge, and financial resources. It is essential to define what that means to your business. If the SEC were to ask why you consider an individual to be a sophisticated investor, you could point to your definition. For example, your ideal sophisticated investor could be a CFO, CPA, accountant, business owner, banker, etc.

BECOMING A SOPHISTICATED INVESTOR

Almost always, a sophisticated investor is a wealthy individual or institution. Capital is generally accepted as a substitute for sophistication because it signifies the individual (or institution) has the skills necessary to amass wealth and has a higher tolerance for loss. Someone with significant experience could have little capital, or someone with substantial wealth could have relatively little market knowledge.

SUMMARY

Accredited investors get access to more investment offerings and opportunities than non-accredited investors. Individuals looking for deals will likely come across opportunities for accredited investors only. Keep in mind that this is for regulation and compliance purposes. There are plenty of investment opportunities available for non-accredited or "sophisticated" investors.

The
Apartment
Queen

We are looking for more investors like you.

**Please complete The Apartment Queen™
Investor Questionnaire to be added to
our list for events and deals:**
https://form.jotform.com/200207883604451

Our ideal investor is typically one of these following
Ultimate passive investors:
WOMEN with 1031 Exchange over $400K
High Net Worth Individuals
Doctors
Dentists
Engineers
Individual with 10 Years' Experience at a Company
Real Estate Brokers/Agents
Female Athletes
Aggie Women
Women CEO, Founder
Socialites
Duchess/Heiress
Individuals with Pension Funds
Endowments
Women-owned Family Offices
Those with Funds Who Support the Social Initiative
to Teach Financial Literacy to Women
Angel Investors Supporting Women

CHAPTER 10 – THE INS AND OUTS OF REAL ESTATE CAPITALIZATION RATES

To be successful in residential real estate investments, you must have a firm grasp of certain financial concepts. Understanding the formulas and metrics can be overwhelming. Not every calculation can help you determine if an investment is right for you. However, knowing how and when to use different valuation tools will help you know which method works best.

CAPITALIZATION RATE ("CAP RATE")

The Cap Rate varies depending on the property asset type. Multi-family properties typically have the lowest average cap rates because they have a lower financial risk. Investors commonly use the Cap Rate to measure the investment potential of a property because it shows the estimated annual rate of return (the loss or gain on an investment).

The most common way to calculate the cap rate is:

Cap Rate = (Net Operating Income) / (Current Fair Market Value)

1. NET OPERATING INCOME (NOI)

NOI is the gross rental income (the total amount of money you receive from rent) minus operating expenses (payroll, repairs, taxes, utilities, etc.).

NOI = Income - Expenses

CURRENT FAIR MARKET VALUE

Use either the asking price or your offer price.

Property List Price – $800,000
Estimated annual operating expenses – $25,000.
Estimated annual income – $100,000
Estimated NOI: $100,000 - $25,000 = $75,000

CAP RATE

$$\$75,000/\$800,000 = 9.4\%.$$

The cap rate calculation above assumes you will receive full rent each month and that the property is 100% occupied 365 days of the year, which is unlikely for a multifamily building with frequent turnover. So, whenever possible, you should adjust for an occupancy rate of less than 100% when calculating your cap rate using the following formula:

Net Operating Income =
[(Gross Rental Income) x **(Occupancy Rate)**] – (Operating Expenses)

Most investors factor a 5-10% loss of rent into their calculations. A 90% occupancy in the above the example would give you the following:

Net operating income = [($100,000) x (.90)] - $25,000 = $65,000.

Adjusted Cap Rate = $65,000/$8000,000 = 8.1%

CAP RATE FOR MULTIFAMILY INVESTING

Calculating the cap rate is helpful when you're assessing a property from which you expect to yield a relatively predictable income, such as a 4-unit apartment building occupied by tenants with year-long leases.

Comparing the cap rates of two similar properties in the same area can help you decide which property is a better addition to your portfolio.

Finally, knowing the cap rate for a potential investment property can help you determine if the asking price is reasonable or if you should negotiate a lower price. (**Note:** To calculate the price you would be willing to pay for a particular property, you can divide your calculated net income by your target cap rate.)

The "cap rate" you should buy at depends on the property location and the return you require to make the investment worth it to you. For example, investors may purchase properties in high-demand (and less risky) areas at a 4% cap rate but hold out for at least a 10% cap rate for low-demand areas.

WHEN KNOWING THE CAP RATE ISN'T SO HELPFUL

Knowing the cap rate for a property that you are planning to flip, rent out on a short-term basis, or offer as a vacation rental isn't very useful. Investors who plan to flip a property want to hold onto it for only a short time, making the cap rate's 12-month frame of reference less relevant.

Vacation and short-term rentals will likely experience fluctuations in income, occupancy, and operating expenses that vary due to seasonal maintenance or repairs resulting from high tenant turnover. Since these factors affect your NOI, they result in an unreliable cap rate calculation.

Important: The cap rate calculation assumes you are paying cash for the property and does not include any costs associated with a mortgage (i.e., interest, points, etc., or other costs of acquiring the property, such as brokers' fees and closing costs.

IMPORTANCE OF CAP RATE TO MULTIFAMILY INVESTORS

The three main benefits of calculating the cap rate for a multifamily property are:

Level of Risk – The cap rate is inversely related to the risk involved. Properties with a lower cap rate have less risk but may not be a good investment. A higher cap rate indicates a higher potential ROI and a higher risk. Investors must determine the sweet spot that balances risk and reward.

Analyze and Screen Potential Investments – Real estate investors use the cap rate as a baseline metric when comparing multiple properties and is one of the first things they review when investigating new investments in multifamily properties.

Calculating ROI – The main benefit of using cap rates is the ability to project a return-on-investment using the data available.

GOOD CAP RATE FOR MULTIFAMILY INVESTMENTS

Typically, a good cap rate for a multifamily property investment is between 4% and 10%.

However, the cap rate is only a useful metric if you are comparing similar investments. Three major factors must be considered: **asset type**, **asset class**, and **location**.

1. ASSET TYPE AND CAP RATE

Cap rates vary depending on the property you are evaluating because the level of perceived risk differs among asset types. Multifamily properties have low average cap rates due to their low financial risk.

2. ASSET CLASS AND CAP RATE

Within the multifamily asset class, properties are graded by quality, mainly driven by age and upkeep. Age is the simplest way to grade investments when comparing cap rate.

Asset class helps better compare properties of similar value to one another based upon the overall integrity and age of a property. A general breakdown of multifamily property asset classes is as follows:

Class A – Less than 10 years old

Class B – 10-20 years old

Class C – 20-30 years old

Class D – 30+ years old

Class A multifamily properties have the lowest cap rates because newly-constructed properties have less risk and higher property value

3. LOCATION AND CAP RATE

The location of an asset can directly affect the cap rate. Properties in less desirable locations will have higher cap rates, and properties in more desirable areas will have lower cap rates.

Chapter 11 – Adding Value to Force Appreciation

Instead of waiting for a property to appreciate organically over time, we can force appreciation by adding value to the property, increasing our Net Operating Income. Calculate the impact of the forced appreciation as follows:

Current Market Value = Net Operating Income/Cap Rate

Let's say you increase the net rents by $10 per unit on a 50-unit complex at a compressed capitalization rate[1] of 8. The property's value would increase by $75,000 in just one year.

Listed below are some ways a property owner can increase NOI to force appreciation in one (1) to four (4) years:

Utilities. Use a Ratio Utility Billing System (RUBS) to allocate utility expenses to the tenants to provide property owners some insulation against increasing utility costs that negatively impact NOI. Using a RUBS is an excellent alternative to increasing rents.

Application fees. Pass on the costs for credit and background checks to prospective tenants.

Returned check fees or late fees. Recoup any expenses incurred from returned checks and establish late fees for residents who do not pay rent on time.

Pet fees. Collect non-refundable deposits for all pets living at the property.

---

[1] When investors believe that prices will continue to rise in rising markets and will pay more for a property with no underlying changes in the market, prices increase and CAP rates fall, creating CAP rate compression.

Pet Rent. Increase monthly rents by a certain amount for each pet living in a unit.

Parking Fees. Most multifamily complexes have enough parking spaces for each tenant, but you can charge additional fees for reserved parking spots.

Cable TV Service and Fees. Cable service adds significant value to each unit. Tenants consider units with cable TV as a premium, which can increase your forced appreciation.

Facilities fees. Many complexes possess good and grand amenities. Fees for using these can also increase your NOI and add value to your multifamily complex.

Laundry Facilities. The majority of multifamily complexes offer laundry facilities that residents can use for a fee.

Low flow toilet, shower heads, faucet aerators. Installing these fixtures can reduce the water bill for an entire complex by 10%.

Curb appeal. This will not instantly translate into money but can generate more traffic, leading to increased occupancy and reduced advertising expenses.

Upgrades on each unit. Depending on the type of market, upgrades and renovations can increase rents per unit.

Office. It is imperative always to upgrade the office one notch higher than the complex itself. It is the first thing prospective tenants see when they come to the property. A comfortable, cozy, classy, sophisticated office with freshly baked cookies and hot coffee will entice visitors to rent.

Wasted space. If you have some unused space, add value by adding more units.

Amenities. All "Class A" type complexes should have amenities such as a clubhouse, gym, benches, playground, pool chairs, and barbeque grills. All other property classes should have amenities that meet the needs of their tenants and are similar to other properties in the surrounding area.

Exterior Renovations. Renovating the building's exterior is similar to curb-appeal as it makes the property more enticing to prospective tenants. The more security you incorporate, the better. If residents feel safe living there, they will stay longer, reducing vacancies and turnover costs.

Vacancy and Economic Loss. You may lose money when there is a vacancy or non-payment of rents by tenants. Monitor this closely every month. If your tenants are not paying on time, find out how your property manager handles this.

The 3: Always confirm the income requirement with current pay stubs, and prospective tenants should have good credit (it doesn't have to be excellent). You may collect an additional month's rent as a deposit in the event of a missed payment. By the third of the month, late fees begin to accrue, and the tenant receives an eviction notice.

Utilize one internet provider and one energy broker. This can add value and additional income to the complex.

The above are just a few examples of actions you can take to generate more income while adding value to each unit.

The **Apartment** *Queen*

We are looking for more investors like you.

**Please complete The Apartment Queen™
Investor Questionnaire to be added to
our list for events and deals:**
https://form.jotform.com/200207883604451

Our ideal investor is typically one of these following

Ultimate passive investors:
WOMEN with 1031 Exchange over $400K
High Net Worth Individuals
Doctors
Dentists
Engineers
Individual with 10 Years' Experience at a Company
Real Estate Brokers/Agents
Female Athletes
Aggie Women
Women CEO, Founder
Socialites
Duchess/Heiress
Individuals with Pension Funds
Endowments
Women-owned Family Offices
Those with Funds Who Support the Social Initiative
to Teach Financial Literacy to Women
Angel Investors Supporting Women

Chapter 12 – Negotiation Strategies Every Multifamily Real Estate Investor Should Know

As an investor, your ability to close the deal directly impacts your income, so it is a skill you want to master. Finding deals is only the first step in the process. Next, you must negotiate with the other side to find common ground beneficial to both parties. Generally, one or more parties must compromise or settle on mutually agreeable points.

Being familiar with your local market will help you develop your negotiation strategy because you will know what works and what doesn't for the area. Also, you will know immediately if an offer is too low.

Because of the potential hundreds of variables involved in a sales transaction, you can adapt the purchase contract to best position yourself for negotiations. Property price, closing date, seller credits, and financing contingency periods for contractual items such as loan qualification, property inspections, and property appraisals can all be modified.

If you want to become a better negotiator, read through the strategies listed below:

1. Create a solution for all partners involved
2. Be prepared, willing, and able to walk away from the deal
3. Include an escalation clause
4. Be informed
5. Handle negotiations in person
6. Listen carefully to the conversation at hand

Win/Win Negotiations

The key to achieving a win-win solution when negotiating is understanding that value comes in more forms than just money. A good negotiator can find common ground and areas in which each party can compromise.

Some typical concessions that either party can make that also have significant value when negotiating the final sale prices are listed below:

Settlement period: The length of time for settlement is not fixed and can be negotiated. For example, it can be as short as two weeks and can run longer to meet both parties' needs.

Financing or Paying Cash: If you can pay cash and avoid any potential issues with financing, you may be able to use that to your benefit.

Repairs: Consider the number of repairs needed when negotiating the price of a property. If the seller doesn't budge on the sale price, they may be willing to make some repairs.

Fees and Closing Costs: There are numerous fees to be paid when purchasing a property. It's worth discussing who will be responsible for paying the fees.

The negotiation process must conclude with both parties feeling that they have won.

BE PREPARED TO WALK AWAY

Before entering into any negotiation, you must determine if you are willing to walk away and be comfortable doing that.

Sometimes the deals you negotiate but don't complete are the most profitable. Don't continue to negotiate a deal if the outcome won't be beneficial.

Be careful not to default to a level slightly above your pre-determined walk-away point. Ideally, you want to reach an agreement that is nowhere close to your walk-away point.

If the other party senses that you will not actually walk away, they will aggressively push you to give them a better deal.

Your goal should never be to have to walk away from a deal. However, if it's necessary, you must be able to do it confidently.

ESCALATION CLAUSE

An escalation clause within a real estate contract indicates that the buyer is willing and able to increase their original offer if subsequent higher offers are submitted. Essentially, this offers a safety net to prospective buyers who are outbid by another party.

Escalator clauses convey two very important messages to the seller:

1. It is a serious offer

2. How far the buyer is willing to go.

Escalation clauses typically include a cap indicating exactly how high the potential buyer is willing to go. A more specific escalator clause will indicate how much they are willing to go above subsequent offers up to a certain point.

BE KNOWLEDGEABLE ABOUT THE DEAL

Information is power. Ensure you know everything about the property, including the current market conditions, the reasons the seller is selling, and the seller's minimum selling price.

NEGOTIATE IN PERSON

Because one party may not clearly understand the tones and intentions in emails or texts, it is always best to negotiate in person. Avoid the possibility of hurting the other party with a typed comment that was genuinely favorable, neutral, or even meant to be funny.

Make sure that everyone feels positive about the outcome before leaving the room. Shake hands and thank the other parties for their participation.

LISTEN MORE THAN YOU SPEAK

When negotiating, you can't expect the other party to show all their cards upfront. It's essential that you ask questions throughout the negotiation process and, more importantly, listen carefully. Actively listening allows you to build rapport, understanding, and trust. The information you obtain will also provide insight into the other party's interests, allowing you to create options, solutions, and win-win agreements.

Some techniques you can use to show that you are interested in what the other person is saying are as follows:

- Use brief conversation prompts to show you're listening, but don't interrupt.

- Paraphrase what the other party says in your own words.

- Ask questions to clarify what the other person is saying and draw more information from them.

- Take advantage of the silence.

- Maintain eye contact and avoid distraction while the other person is talking. Nod occasionally to show agreement.

- Provide feedback.

Active listening shows that you care about what the other person has to say.

CONCLUSION

Negotiating skills, techniques, and strategies will be valuable in many areas of your life. If you commit to learning, developing, and mastering these skills, you will develop a more effective means of communication that you can apply in business and personal relationships.

The best negotiators possess patience and respect, which are essential to turn an average negotiator into a skilled and accomplished negotiator.

CHAPTER 13 – RAISING PRIVATE CAPITAL FROM OTHER PEOPLE'S IRAs

Disclaimer:

The Apartment Queen does not provide tax, legal, or investment advice or endorse any products, services or investments of any type.

All information and materials are for educational purposes only. All parties are encouraged to consult with their attorneys, accountants, and financial advisors before entering into any type of investment.

When investors need funding for deals, there are several options available. Funds for multifamily syndication and commercial deals often come from individuals' IRAs because it allows them to be completely passive while investing in real estate.

If you plan to use other people's retirement funds for your investments, be sure to do your due diligence and work only with professional IRA custodians.

Self-directed IRA custodians must remain neutral. You can't call them and say, "Hey, can you send me a list of all of your clients who are looking for an investment?"

They cannot send you that information, but most have several resources available and offer training on starting the conversation and what you should know.

WHY RAISE CAPITAL FROM OTHER PEOPLE'S IRAs

As a real estate investor, some of your projects may not qualify for traditional bank loans. Hard money kind can be expensive. However, hard money can be an excellent option for a new investor because hard money lenders will not loan on a bad deal.

Another option is to use private capital from other people's IRAs to fund your project. Unlike traditional banks, the process is generally quick. If the funds are already there, some custodians can fund a deal in 24 to 48 hours from the time the investment documents are received.

Because these loans relationship-based, loan terms, such as interest rate and equity appreciation, can vary depending on how the lender and borrower choose to structure the deal.

Currently, there are trillions of dollars in American retirement accounts (IRAs and 401ks), and Americans are not happy with the returns they're making. People are getting smarter; they're tired of the ups and downs of the stock market and are starting to move their funds to self-directed IRAs so that they can invest in non-traditional assets.

This could be a really great way to securely invest your money into a completely different class of assets.

If you're looking for ways to raise money from other people's IRAs, ask them, "How are your retirement returns? Are you happy with them? Do you have a plan to for retirement by moving some of your money out of the stock market and into assets, such as notes, promissory notes secured by real estate, private placement investments, or physical real estate? These are tangible assets that are not going to disappear one day like the stock market.

With the global pandemic, some people lost 20-30% of their retirement funds in a matter of two to three days. And you ultimately have no control over that. So, if you're looking to use money from other people's IRAs, really use that selling point to your advantage.

Many people are looking for alternative investment options because they have undirected cash sitting in their IRA accounts. That cash will not grow until the account holders choose somewhere to invest it. There's a lot of capital out there waiting for the right conversation to happen.

RAISING PRIVATE CAPITAL BASICS

TYPES OF ACCOUNTS THAT CAN BE SELF-DIRECTED

Seven types of accounts can be self-directed, and they all have various benefits. Also, there is no limit to how many IRAs an individual can have. So, as you're looking to raise private capital from these accounts, you need a solid foundation of how these accounts work, how the money can move around, and other basic rules.

Some individuals are *disqualified people*, meaning you cannot use their IRA funds for your feal. For example, you can't use your spouse's account or your own IRA to fund your investment. Make sure you are aware of the restrictions when investing with your own IRA or raising money from other people's IRAs as well.

If you're talking with someone who has their retirement savings in a 401k account, always ask if they are still employed where their 401k or other retirement account is. Typically, those accounts are not eligible to be rolled over into an IRA until that individual no longer works at that company.

Keep in mind that although your custodian may have a very fast turnaround time, they cannot control the time required by other custodians. When someone opens a self-directed IRA, it can take three to five business days to three to five weeks to move the funds from the current custodian. Give yourself enough time to move the funds over to invest in your deal ultimately.

DOCUMENTATION

It's important to understand that the individual is not investing; their IRA is. Passive investors will expect you to know how this process works. Be proactive and find out what the IRA custodian will need. Show that you are a knowledgeable and credible party to anyone investing their retirement money in your deal.

Find a custodian who makes information easily available (for example, lists all of the instructions on their website) and has transaction specialists based on the types of investments that they fund.

HOW TO RAISE PRIVATE CAPITAL

First, you have to build a network and make connections. Attend in-person or virtual meetups to find investors. You also need to know how to introduce the conversation with a basic overview of the process, then bring the IRA custodian into the conversation.

IRA custodians are always neutral. They do not recommend or endorse individuals or investments. From a completely impartial standpoint, a representative will educate potential investors who are interested in using their IRA to invest with you, including:

- Logistics
- How funds move back and forth
- Tax consequences
- Opening an account
- Fees

It is your responsibility to proceed ethically with good intentions, showing credibility through references. Let investors know how their investment will be protected if the worst-case scenario occurs.

Be prepared to show the numbers, stats, returns, and contingency plans if something goes south.

In this business, reputation and ethics are everything. If you are screwing over your investors, know that word travels fast. Protect your investors because that will ultimately attract other investors to help build and maintain a solid reputation.

MAKE YOUR DEALS GO SMOOTHLY

Once you find investors, follow through and do your part to ensure the deal goes smoothly.

Your IRA specialist cannot provide tax, legal, or investment advice, so you need other professionals in your network for things like statutory compliance. Also, stay informed of the overall structure of your deal and understand the timeframes. You don't want to find out three weeks before a deal needs to be funded that your potential investor does not want to move that fast.

Allow your investors enough time to evaluate the deal, evaluate their options, open an account, move the funds, and fund the investment. IMPORTANT: Investors must submit funds to the custodian. Do not tell your investors to wire $50,000 from their IRA to your bank account.

Provide the wiring instructions to the investor with the investment documents showing the IRA taking the investment title. Once the client signs the necessary documents for the investment, many custodians can fund the deal in 24 to 48 hours. Sometimes revisions to the paperwork are required, so add extra days to the process to be safe.

Continually update your investors on the progress and inform them when distributions are sent. Communication helps reinforce your reputation.

ANNUAL REPORTING REQUIREMENTS

IRA custodians are required to report the value of their clients' assets to the IRS once per year. Investors hold all types of assets in their IRAs: properties, raw land entity, investment notes, etc., making it difficult to determine and absolute value for that asset. As a result, clients are required to report the Fair Market Valuation (FMV) for their assets with supporting documentation.

Notices go out in November or December, because the fair market values are due January 15th. If you are a syndicator with five to 20 IRA investors, put all account numbers in a spreadsheet with their corresponding values to send to your IRA custodian.

Make sure that you're aware of this otherwise all of your IRA investors will be calling you on January 14th after discovering you have not submitted this.

If the custodian does not receive this information after sending several messages, they will distribute the asset because at that point, it's administratively unfeasible. However, that's the worst-case scenario. Typically, the client will call asking how to submit the information when they receive the final notice.

And again, integrity is important when dealing with other people's retirement money. Unfortunately, people lose money sometimes. You could lose money in a real estate deal if you don't invest with the right person.

On the flip side, if you invest with your IRA, do your due diligence and your research. Don't just Google a name. Include qualifiers like fraud, court cases, bad reviews. For example, "Joe Smith Fraud." Doing this will help protect you in the long run.

NEXT STEPS

Now that you know how you can introduce the conversation, you need to know how IRAs work to show investors that you're knowledgeable. Many investors first learn about self-directed IRAs from someone who wants them to invest $100,000 in their new deal.

Likely, they will want to know more about the process, the custodian, and whether the funds are FDIC-insured.

Find a custodian to work with who answers your calls, knows about the types of deals you're doing, and understands the rules and restrictions for investing with IRAs.

Before opening an account, sit down with an IRA specialist who will walk you through the process. Whether you're looking to invest with your own IRA or raise capital from other people's IRAs for your deals, it is critical to have a good relationship with your IRA custodian.

Build that relationship with a custodian who aligns with your goals and expected customer service requirements.

LEADING LADIES IN MULTIFAMILY REAL ESTATE

If you are a female interested in becoming a real estate investor, read the following stories to see how other successful investors got their start.

Chapter 14 – Sara Laschever: Author of "Women Don't Ask"

Sara Laschever is an internationally-recognized authority on the obstacles women confront in the workplace. She is the co-author of "Women Don't Ask" and "Ask For It: How Women Can Use the Power of Negotiation to Get What They Really Want."

In this chapter, Sara shares why "women don't ask" and offers some tips and strategies women can use during negotiations for any industry.

Introduction

"Women Don't Ask" is a serious work of social science as well as a very accessible, easy-to-read book built on a very strong research foundation, written by Linda Babcock and Sara Laschever. Babcock, a behavioral economist, conducted several studies using different methodologies and found that men typically ask for things for themselves that will help them get ahead four times as frequently as women.

These requests for opportunities, access to resources, etc., help men edge ahead up the ladder a little faster and a little sooner than women. There are several good reasons why women are nervous about asking for more and why they avoid it but women pay a high price for not asking for what they want and not advocating for themselves.

One of the primary reasons that women don't ask is they worry it will elicit a backlash. People don't like it when women come off as too aggressive. There are several ways women can ask for what they want without coming off as pushy, bossy, threatening, or demanding.

Many of the concepts in the book talk about other women being around each other. Because we're collaborative, our efforts are able to help us to have more success in groups of us instead of being the token woman in a male-dominated industry.

PREPARATION IS KEY

In a serious negotiation where the stakes are high, preparation is critical. Do your research and find out what other people are asking for and getting. Look outside your organization to competitors in allied fields where you might be marketable.

If you're really nervous about it, especially if you're worried that others will think you are coming on too strong, get together with somebody you trust and do some role play. Brief them thoroughly about the negotiation and your concerns. Play it through several times and get them to push your buttons, embarrass you, make you mad, and hurt your feelings. Practice responding in calm ways that move the conversation away from conflict towards joint problem solving. If both parties are far apart in negotiations, keep talking until you find some middle ground.

Although it may feel awkward, if you practice what to say in advance, you will be much better prepared and won't be caught off guard by emotional triggers where you're embarrassed, angry, or your feelings are hurt. If you prepare and trigger those emotions during role play, it's much easier to see them for what they are. Put them to the side and just keep going.

If you're not somebody who feels like you're good on your feet, consider taking an improv class. Many improv companies do business training in organizations because it involves the ability to pivot in a focused, calm way and understand what is necessary to get you to feel loose on your feet. So, whatever gets thrown at you, even if you're not prepared, you can decide what to say.

TIPS TO PREPARE FOR CONVERSATIONS

If you get asked a question that you are unsure how to answer, ask, "Can we take a quick break?" or "Can we pick this up in a couple of hours?" Take a few minutes to research any topics that you didn't expect. Don't make hasty decisions.

Also, don't hesitate to ask for clarification or for someone to restate a question or comment, which gives you some time to regroup your thoughts. If you ask questions from a couple of different angles, you'll get a little more information, or the respondent will reveal something they are willing to do.

If you have a past experience that is preventing them from hearing the benefits of your proposal because they're hung up on something that isn't relevant, take the time to talk it through.

Finally, suggest you care about their situation by saying things like, Tell me what's going on with you. What are your problems? What issues are holding you back? How can I help? Instead of This is what I want. This is my position, come to me. Show that you are an ally and can work together to solve problems.

HAVING DIFFICULT CONVERSATIONS YOUR EMPLOYER

Preparation is really important. Find out if A) other people have gotten what you're asking for in the past, or B), there is a sudden budget influx to ramp up projects related to what you want to do. Also, talk to the executive assistants in their department. They may have some pointers, such as, *Do it this way*, or *He responds really well to…*

Doing your research is great, but you still may hit a roadblock. If the conversation isn't flowing, you might say, "I would really love it if you could think about it…" Then say, "Maybe we could talk again tomorrow."

The other party might then reflect on your request and realize that would be good for business, the department, and performance targets. It also shows that you're calm.

Finally, if you do the research, bring the data with you to the meeting to increase their understanding of what you're saying and try to meet you somewhere. If you can find agreement on one small piece, that increases the incentive to keep going to reach a final agreement of some sort.

You may need to yield on something small that isn't that important to you but gives the other negotiator a win. There's a common psychological dynamic where people reciprocate when they feel they've been given something.

NO DOESN'T ALWAYS MEAN NO

Sara's dad always said to her and her siblings, "Don't take no for an answer the first three times." Doing so may cause people to say, "What about 'no' don't you understand?" The thing is: NO is often just an opening gambit or it's based on inaccurate or insufficient information. Or it's a *no maybe*. Life is more negotiable than many believe, especially in the Western world where a lot of us assume that the price is the price. When there's a sticker or a tag, buyers are not as inclined to say, "Well, let's talk about the money. Maybe we can make it work."

That's a really important lesson. Don't accept "no" as an answer early in a conversation.

OTHER NEGOTIATION RESOURCES

If you live in a city where there's a business school, take an executive course that will allow you to practice negotiating over 12-13 weeks for a few hours per week. In this setting, you will experience many different scenarios with people you don't know very well. It's a great investment in yourself.

Many schools have online programs, such as the Harvard Program on Negotiation, the Harvard Kennedy School, the Harvard Business School, and also MIT Sloan School. Other schools offer week-long adult camps where you can learn about negotiation, business leadership, and useful topics.

Some great books about negotiation are as follows:

"Shadow Negotiation" by Debra Kolb and Judith Williams

"What Works: Gender Equality by Design" by Iris Bohnet

"What Works for Women at Work: Four Patterns Working Women Need to Know" by Joan C. Williams and Rachel Dempsey

"Never Split the Difference: Negotiating As If Your Life Depended On It" by Chris Voss and Tahl Raz

"Getting to Yes: Negotiating Agreement Without Giving In" by Roger Fisher, William L. Ury, and Bruce Patton

SOCIAL COSTS

The social costs of not utilizing women's skills, energy, imagination, and creativity are huge. Women tend to reinvest their money into their communities more than men do, which is another reason for equal pay. Women invest in taking care of their families.

For any society to be successful, it must raise healthy, productive citizens, which is something women typically do more than men. It's important to note that these women are not anti-men and don't blame men for any inequalities. Men are the products of the same socialization as women. They also have had a lot of noise in their ears about what men do and what women do and how they may not be the same.

Many men are eager to be great leaders for everybody in an organization and want to know where the talent is, so they can promote it.

Millennial men tend to want a lot of what women have always wanted—more time with their families. They don't want to work like the boomer dads who were gone 90 hours a week and could never come to their soccer games. They want more time for their hobbies and causes and want more balance in their lives.

Most millennial men have grown up with grandmothers, mothers, sisters, aunts, cousins, friends, and wives who work. To them, it's normal for lots of women to be around and they're happy to help promote the ones who are. So, go millennials!

WOMEN IN THE WORKPLACE

Women having children and returning to work shouldn't be perceived as a liability. Also, a young woman shouldn't miss out on an opportunity because she may have a child in the future.

Things will change when high-quality state-sponsored childcare is available. When women know that their families are well cared for, they are happy to go back to work and put their whole selves into it.

Also, there is a need for more social support for working women and for greater balance. The recent pandemic revealed a lot about how women balance work and home with their partners. Even with the best intentions, when push comes to shove and there's really an emergency, women tend to pick up more of the slack.

However, that is changing with millennial men. Perceived ideas about masculinity and what it means are pretty loud in people's ears. Being a breadwinner, being super successful, and making that your number one priority is not a strong message that women get.

But as women start to get more social support, it will seem normal.

GETTING STARTED

Sara met Linda at that critical moment when Linda was looking for a non-academic writer. Linda's ideas really aligned with Sara's childhood conditioning. Linda had insight into her graduate students. She saw first-hand that male graduate students would say, "Hey, I need this. Can you help me with that? Are there funds and resources for such and such?"

The women would say, "How can you give it to him? I would love to have that. Why couldn't I have it?" Linda would reply, "Well, you didn't ask. He asked."

So she recognized this difference between the approach men and women took to ask for help. She was very interested in negotiation and decided to see if there was more to it than what she was seeing.

Women own or are majority owners in about 40% of the private businesses in this country, but only get a small percentage of the investment capital from angel investors. To a significant degree, it's because women don't ask for enough, don't ask at all, or ask only for the bare minimum they think is needed to get going.

So, women's businesses are often under-capitalized, which creates stress, and puts the business, employees, and the community where those employees live at risk.

Men ask for more and get more. Ladies go in and ask for more, too.

PRACTICE ASKING

In their second book, "Ask For It," Sara and Linda devised the *negotiation gym* to strengthen your negotiating muscles. During the six-week program, each week you will focus on a different challenge or difficulty that women in particular run into when they're trying to negotiate.

You will be sent out to negotiate low-stakes deals that will not make or break your career. For example, in mid-September, summer merchandise is still in your favorite boutique and you've had your eye on something that's not marked down quite enough. Ask, "Could you give it to me for 20% less?" Or try buying tomatoes in bulk at a Farmer's Market. Try negotiating little things and you will be surprised how many things are negotiable that you didn't think were.

In the last downturn in 2008, it was widely reported that several big box stores quietly told their associates, "If a customer tries to negotiate, we'd rather sell the air conditioner or refrigerator than have them walk out and buy it somewhere else."

Next, the program will push you to ask for twice as much as you think you can get. This will surprise you and is a really good lesson that you're aiming too low. Aim higher. Ask for things you think it's not okay to ask for because you're a nice girl.

Sara's favorite week is when women ask for things they know they absolutely cannot get because they fear hearing "No." Research shows that men's self-esteem is more stable. Women's self-esteem fluctuates more in response to praise, criticism, success, or failure.

We're afraid of NO so we don't ask at all. So, it's a great exercise for women to ask for something and hear, "Nope." This shows them they will survive even if they are turned down.

One summer when gas prices were sky high, Linda tried to negotiate the cost of a tank of gas with a 7-11 employee. He laughed at her and she went back to her graduate students and said, "He laughed at me. I'm okay."

Women working through the negotiation gym program often work with a gym buddy for accountability. Buddies keep each other honest, debrief one another, and work together to ask for more, which can also make it more fun.

ABOUT SARA LASCHEVER

A leading authority on the challenges that shape women's lives and careers, Sara Laschever is the co-author, with Linda Babcock, of the groundbreaking books "Women Don't Ask: The High Cost of Avoiding Negotiation—and Positive Strategies for Change" and "Ask for It! How Women Can Use the Power of Negotiation to Get What They Really Want." She has written extensively about women in business, women in literature and the arts, women in academia, and women in the sciences. Her work has been published by The New York Times, The Harvard Business Review, The Guardian, The New York Review of Books, Vogue, Glamour, and many other publications.

Sara worked as a research associate and principal interviewer for Project Access, a landmark Harvard University study that explored impediments to women's careers in science, and is a founding faculty member of the Carnegie Mellon Leadership and Negotiation Academy for Women. She also served as Senior Fellow at the Center for Work-

Life Policy (now the Center for Talent Innovation) and as academic coordinator for the Inaugural WIN Summit, a national conference focused on helping women learn to negotiate.

Sara Laschever earned her bachelor's degree (*summa cum laude*) from Princeton University and a master's degree from Boston University. She lives in Concord, Massachusetts.

CONTACT SARA

Website
SaraLaschever.com

The Apartment *Queen*

We are looking for more investors like you.

Please complete The Apartment Queen™ Investor Questionnaire to be added to our list for events and deals:
https://form.jotform.com/200207883604451

Our ideal investor is typically one of these following
Ultimate passive investors:
WOMEN with 1031 Exchange over $400K
High Net Worth Individuals
Doctors
Dentists
Engineers
Individual with 10 Years' Experience at a Company
Real Estate Brokers/Agents
Female Athletes
Aggie Women
Women CEO, Founder
Socialites
Duchess/Heiress
Individuals with Pension Funds
Endowments
Women-owned Family Offices
Those with Funds Who Support the Social Initiative
to Teach Financial Literacy to Women
Angel Investors Supporting Women

CHAPTER 15 – KELLY STINSON: SAVE WATER, SAVE MONEY

In any business, reducing expenses helps to improve cash flow and, ultimately, profitability. For multifamily properties, reducing costs can increase your cash flow and enable you to later sell the property for more than competing properties.

It is important to minimize a property's expenses because they directly impact the Net Operating Income (NOI). *The NOI is calculated by subtracting the total expenses from the total revenue.*

Buyers and sellers use the Capitalization Rate, referred to as the "cap rate," as a benchmark to establish a property's value. Cap rates are determined by supply and demand and will be similar for two identical buildings in the same area.

Typically, a property with a higher NOI will sell for more than a nearby property with a lower NOI.

LET'S TALK TOILETS

Kelly Stinson, "The Potty Princess," shares water conservation methods and ways to increase value in your multifamily investment.

It's not a sexy topic and can be a little uncomfortable. But it can save us a lot of money, so let's have some fun with it.

You can attribute 24% of indoor water usage for a multifamily property to toilets. As an asset owner, you need to understand how interior fixture flow rates will impact the water/sewer expense line on the **T12**. The greater the consumption, the higher the cost.

> **What is a T12?**
>
> T12 is the Trailing Twelve Financials on a property that lists all of the income and expenses, as well as the Net Operating Income (NOI).
>
> **NOI = Total Income – Total Expenses**
>
> Note: a T6 would include information for the past six months, a T3 for the past three months, and a T1* would be for the last 30 days.
>
> *During the 2020 pandemic, the T1 helped provide very specific information.

WATER CONSERVATION FIXTURES

Commercial properties such as apartments, multifamily homes, senior living facilities, and hotels use a lot of resources. On average, each of us flushes a toilet three to five times per day. Because of the recent pandemic, people stay at home more, resulting in a consumption increase of three to five times more for some residential multifamily properties. That water usage was previously spread out amongst the various locations we would visit throughout the day.

To help conserve water (and reduce costs), property owners can install ultra-high-efficiency plumbing fixtures on toilets, shower heads, kitchen faucets, and bathroom faucets.

Let's look at an example:

200-unit property

$50,000 investment

$50,000 saved in water and sewer expenses in the first year

Asset Value boost of $769,000 (if you're running it at a 6.5 cap rate).

Saving water results in increased cash flow, and that makes investors happy. The bigger the property, the more impact it has on your income.

Be aware that the impact can vary depending on the water and sewer rates for the area in which the property is located. These rates fluctuate across the country. For example, in Tulsa, the sewer rate is three times the water rate. Other locations, like in Ohio, send separate bills for water and sewer. *So when looking at a T-12, consider that a sewer expense may be associated with the interior water usage.*

WHEN TO UPGRADE

Not every property is an ideal candidate for a water conservation project, or it may not fit in your particular business plan. It depends on how long you're going to hold the asset and what you're trying to accomplish.

When doing your due diligence, keep in mind that no property is the same as a property across the street.

If the toilets in the property have been upgraded, your first question should be, "Are they running efficiently?" Not every toilet is created equal. Sometimes, toilets are placed into applications, and the water usage increases because the waste is not being pushed down the line. Residents must double flush, or the flappers will corrode over time, creating silent leaks in the toilet.

If the toilets haven't been upgraded, determine how old they are. Have they been maintained? Are they three-and-a-half gallons per flush toilets? If you're going to hold the property for three to five years, it will make sense to replace the older toilets, especially if you are rubbing back utility costs to the residents.

Ratio Utility Billback Systems (RUBS)

RUBS is a method used to calculate utility consumption for each tenant in a multifamily community.

Using a RUBS is one of the most cost-effective methods for property managers to transition utility costs to residents and ensure you aren't responsible for an expense that you have nearly no control over as a property owner. By separating utility costs and billing tenants directly, owners can also not only shield themselves from rising utility prices but also increase the value of their property while at the same time benefiting tenants.

SCENARIO 1 – SMALL PROPERTY

- 26 Units
- High-efficiency shower heads installed in all units
- Aerators installed on bathroom and kitchen faucets in all units
- New toilets installed in 13 units
- Rubbing back utility bills (RUBS)

For this property, the owners had already installed most of the water conservation upgrades, including replacing shower heads and aerators in all units, and toilets in half (13 of 26) of the units.

Since the tenants were paying 80% of the water costs through RUBS, the decrease in expenses, and ultimately the NOI, was not significant enough to justify the costs for materials and labor to replace the 13 remaining toilets.

SCENARIO 2 – LARGE PROPERTY

- 100-200 Units
- Master Meter
- Not Rubbing back utility bills (RUBS)

In this situation, it would be appropriate to do a clean sweep, buy all the toilets in bulk to get a discount and install them all at the same time. Then, you'll see a significant change in your expenses.

SCENARIO 3 – PROPERTIES BUILT BEFORE 1995

Any time you are working with a property built before 1995, you should evaluate the condition of the plumbing fixtures.

- How old are they?

- How many work orders are coming in?

- Is it a single-family, multifamily, or hospitality property?

As well as being environmentally conscious, it's also the right thing to do to boost NOI.

SCENARIO 4 – HOTELS

Hotels are completely different financially from multifamily properties. Typically, hotels will do renovations one floor at a time to avoid shutting down the entire hotel or getting negative reviews from guests.

TENANT RENEWALS

When a tenant's lease is up for renewal, they will likely determine if it is cost-effective to move or stay. A competitor with completely upgraded interior plumbing can reduce their rub back to 60% since their water bills decreased significantly. Many residents in some property classes are living paycheck to paycheck, and $20 or $50 per month will be the deciding factor for them.

SUSTAINABILITY SOLUTIONS (SAS)

For properties with 50 or more bathrooms, consider using a turnkey service provider who focuses on water conservation for large or multifamily properties, such as Sustainability Solutions (SAS). A team of experts will visit your property and assess every fixture to make recommendations for improving efficiency.

SAS can install fixtures in 50-60 bathrooms per day. Properties with 150 units or 150 keys can be upgraded very quickly so that you will start to see the benefits in the first full monthly billing cycle.

WATER CONSUMPTION AND LEAK DETECTION SENSORS

In addition to dealing with rising water and sewer rates, property owners must be prepared to stop any leaks that occur. Water is very destructive, so it's critical you deal with any leaks quickly.

There are many incredible options for water consumption and leak detection technology. Some are really expensive ($40,000+), making them cost-prohibitive for typical investors or syndicators.

An alternative, less expensive option is a sensor for your water meter that will sit on the meter, connected to a relay, and plugged into an electrical outlet within 1000 feet. The sensors communicate through a **Lora** signal, one of the most secure cellular signals, since Wi-Fi can be inconsistent.

Within two to four weeks, the sensor begins to learn water consumption and behavior patterns for the property and can provide water consumption analysis in real time down to the one-minute level. If an abnormality is detected, an immediate notification is sent that a leak has been detected.

WATER LEAK WITH NO SENSORS

If there is a large water line break, the water must be shut off quickly to avoid costly damage. For example, in a mid-rise property, the main water line was punctured on the second floor, causing water to flow down through and into the garage. Luckily, the building was constructed slightly slanted so the water could drain.

Still, it required a great deal of remediation. The flooring, padding, and drywall had to be removed and replaced. The only reason it wasn't worse is that residents spotted the water and notified maintenance.

It took almost an hour to completely shut off the water. By that time, the damage was done, and the water bill was extremely high. So, in this case, a sensor could have alerted maintenance to the problem sooner and lessen the amount of damage.

WATER LEAK WITH NO SENSORS

In another smaller property, sensors were installed which identified high water usage during the *Golden Hour* from about 1:30 am to 4:00 am when most residents are sleeping, and water usage is typically inactive. They were able to determine that the flappers on the toilets were leaking. Replacing the flappers resolved the leak and prevented costly water bills.

ABOUT KELLY STINSON

Kelly Stinson, "The Potty Princess," has been in the multifamily and water conservation industry for several years. Her passion is sustainability coupled with increasing NOI for multifamily and hospitality owners, investors, and management firms. She consistently delivers a 30-60% reduction in water and sewer consumption while saving our World's most precious resource "one flush at a time." #ThePottyPrincess

Kelly has achieved success in a primarily male-dominated industry with her commitment to staying informed about industry trends through research. Her industry knowledge allows her to be confident and assertive when communicating with others in the industry. She exudes a positive mindset that draws in more attractive experiences.

CONTACT KELLY

Kelly is proud to a resource for others to call who with questions about water bills, utility providers, or multifamily investing.

If you need a resource for water conservation or want to connect and learn more about multifamily, reach out to Kelly.

Facebook
Facebook.com/kdstinson

LinkedIn
LinkedIn.com/in/ThePottyPrincess/

Website
SASConserve.com

The **Apartment**
Queen

We are looking for more investors like you.

Please complete The Apartment Queen™
Investor Questionnaire to be added to
our list for events and deals:
https://form.jotform.com/200207883604451

Our ideal investor is typically one of these following
Ultimate passive investors:
WOMEN with 1031 Exchange over $400K
High Net Worth Individuals
Doctors
Dentists
Engineers
Individual with 10 Years' Experience at a Company
Real Estate Brokers/Agents
Female Athletes
Aggie Women
Women CEO, Founder
Socialites
Duchess/Heiress
Individuals with Pension Funds
Endowments
Women-owned Family Offices
Those with Funds Who Support the Social Initiative
to Teach Financial Literacy to Women
Angel Investors Supporting Women

Chapter 16 – Kim Stallings, MBA: Protecting Cash-Flowing Assets

Multifamily real estate investments often come with some unforeseen risks. Natural disasters, theft, inclement weather conditions, fire, tenant litigation, etc., are examples of events from which you must protect your assets. The right multifamily insurance should focus primarily on your company's return on investment above anything else.

Kim Stallings, Owner/Agent at Heritage Risk Advisors, shared the basics of multifamily insurance and how you can have peace of mind knowing you are 100% protected.

Coverage

Many investors select multifamily property insurance policies based on premium costs, looking for any way to decrease fixed expenses on a cash-flowing property. It's important you understand what your policy covers and what is excluded from coverage.

If your insurance does not cover your asset adequately, you are left holding the bag when your property incurs a loss. Essentially, you are paying for insurance to be lender-compliant only, instead of taking a calculated approach to transferring risk.

Property insurance is filled with landmines and pitfalls (endorsements) that most investors don't bother to read or even worse, their agents don't show them. Many insurance agents fail to explain policy exclusions or how deductibles and co-insurance really works during a claim scenario.

Multifamily properties incur a lot of claims because:

- People are always moving in or out
- Residents often have visitors
- Swimming Pools
- Roof Damage
- Slips and Falls on the Property

- Fires (kitchen, smoking, BBQs)
- Overflowing drains

Some claims can be incredibly expensive and can literally make or break a deal. Ensure you consider the cost of premiums vs. the cost of being under-insured.

Co-Insurance

Most property insurance policies have a co-insurance clause that requires the owner to carry coverage for a certain percentage of the property's replacement cost value at the time of the loss! Typically coinsurance values are expressed in these percentages - 80%, 90%, or 100%. It's like a deductible, but worse, it's a penalty.

So you need to account and forecast the cost to rebuild your property based on national averages of labor and materials in your market in order to play the coinsurance game properly. Of course in the event of a total loss, coinsurance does not apply, they just pay the value listed on the policy minus the deductible. Insurance carriers **do not care about the tax appraised value, market value, or loan amount**; they have to evaluate the property based on replacing it if it burns to the ground or blows away.

The adjuster looks at the cost to rebuild at the **date of your claim**. You also need to know the current construction costs for materials and labor per foot, which is a moving number. Things occur in the greater macro-economic planet that affect costs, such as free trade agreements or a global pandemic that restricts skilled and unskilled labor and access to materials and their shipping. Supply and demand will also affect the price of labor and materials.

If you are not insured to that coefficient (80%, 90%, 100%), you are penalized for the amount you are under-insured * loss amount. If it is a significant loss, but not a total loss, there can be a hefty penalty. Your claim settlement will be reduced by the amount of your deductible **and** the co-insurance penalty.

The formula to determine whether the amount of insurance you have purchased (the limit of insurance) meets your co-insurance requirement:

**Property Value x Co-insurance Percentage =
Minimum Insurance Amount Required**

Here is an example of how co-insurance works:

Building Value	$1,000,000
Co-insurance Requirement	90%

So, the minimum required amount of insurance is:

1,000,000 * 90% = $900,000

Required Amount of Insurance	$900,000
Actual Amount of Insurance	$450,000
Amount of Loss	$200,000

The coinsurance formula is:

**(Actual Amount of Insurance / Amount of Loss) x Amount of Claim
= Co-insurance Penalty**

Inserting the amounts above in the formula produces the following calculation:

($450,000/$900,000) x $200,000 = $100,000 (plus deductible)

The policyholder must pay, or self-insure, the shortfall of $100,000, and of course, don't forget the deductible!!!!

ENDORSEMENT

Endorsements (also referred to as riders and/or exclusions) can be used to add, remove, exclude, or otherwise alter coverage for an insurance policy.

Each carrier uses different endorsements to be more competitive. Like with your auto insurance, there are options that can be incorporated or removed from the standard policy.

Any provisions added will enhance your coverage. But you may not be aware of the options they take away until you see the complete endorsement list, which is a bulleted list in the middle of a quote. Most people only look at the price because they do not realize that endorsements could make one policy worth paying higher premiums. Or as mentioned previously, their agents offer a terms sheet in lieu of a raw quote so you don't see the endorsement list. It's also important to remember that there are different forms and peril structures on policies that dictate the base coverages that the endorsements add and subtract from. Those coverages are only listed in the full policy, which of course you don't get until after you purchase….. Interesting.

The coverage added or taken away in those endorsements is the meat of what you are purchasing. That is why those provisions are very important. Sometimes they have, clever names, and you cannot tell from just reading them what they do or do not cover.

If your broker does their due diligence, then you will know precisely what your coverages are. And if they have no idea, there is a great chance you are talking to the wrong person. In other words, make sure you speak with an agent who is truly knowledgeable about property insurance.

It's always a good idea to check if the following are not excluded from or have a sub-limit in your property insurance coverage:

- Coverage for assault and battery, firearms, abuse, and molestation

- Marijuana and Cannabis – people sometimes grow on the property. The oils are intrusive, get in air ducts and walls, and can't be remediated easily or inexpensively

- Mold and mold remediation

- Virus, bacteria, and communicable diseases (Ebola, etc.)

DEDUCTIBLES

An insurance deductible is the amount of money that you're responsible for paying before your insurance company will pay you for each insured loss.

For example, let's say your policy includes a $2,500 deductible and a $250,000 limit.

Your property incurs a $50,000 fire loss.

If coinsurance does not apply, your insurer will pay $47,500 ($50,000 - $2,500).

If the loss is subject to coinsurance and you do not have an adequate limit, the insurer will reduce your insured loss by the coinsurance penalty. The insurer will pay the difference between the adjusted loss amount and your $2,500 deductible.

Deductibles are inversely related to the price of the coverage. The higher the deductible, the lower the premium because you are taking more risk and you are transferring less risk to the insurance company. When you purchase a brand new property with no wear and tear, you can save a significant amount of money having a high deductible.

Lower deductibles result in higher premiums because you are transferring more risk to the insurance company.

CONSTRUCTION, OCCUPANCY, PROTECTION, AND EXPOSURE (COPE)

In the property insurance world, carriers look at four different aspects of the property to determine the coverage needed and the price.

C – CONSTRUCTION

Carriers will consider the materials used to build the property. A building built using wood frames with wood sidings will burn to the ground faster than a building with brick siding.

O – OCCUPANCY

Carriers will consider

- The type of occupancy
- The number of occupants
- The ages of all occupants
- Section 8?
- Subsidized students?
- Single-family vs. Multifamily
- Is it an Assisted Living Facility?

A vacant property is more expensive to insure than an occupied property because it represents a greater risk. Vacant properties attract vandalism, theft, squatters, or individuals looking for places to conduct illegal activities.

Also, if an incident such as a burst pipe occurs in a vacant property, a great deal of damage can be done before you are aware, increasing the cost of the claim.

P – PROTECTION

Are any measures in place to protect the property from an event happening? For example, are smoke detectors, carbon monoxide detectors, and burglar alarms installed? Was the property built with any "green, LEED certified" construction?

Some other parameters to consider are as follows:

- Is it fenced or not fenced?

- Is it well-lit?

- Is it next to a power treatment plant?

- Is it next to a school zone?

- Is it near single-family housing?

- Is it in a concrete jungle with nothing but industrial building and other apartments?

- What level is the fire department – volunteer or PPC 1?

- How quickly will they respond if there is a fire? That lets you know how much of a building could be saved once it catches on fire.

Also, insurance companies will look at the extra four digits in your zip code to see where a property is located. They can obtain crime and weather claim information for that specific area, which is crucial for premium calculation.

E – EXPOSURE

"Exposure" describes the surrounding risk. Apartments are considered as heavier exposure than commercial office buildings because people move in and out of apartments all the time, properties are vacant, and their locations are usually on the outskirts. Some exposure considerations are:

- Near a lake

- Coastal regions

- Fire zone

- Tornado alley

- Flood zone

SUMMARY

There are many risks that cannot be predicted for multifamily property owners and can spell doom for an otherwise worthwhile investment.

Commercial Insurance policies can include perils that protect against damage to building(s), income loss, increases in expenses from ordinance and law and of course 3rd party liability issues.

Weather is the most uncontrollable force. Think hail damage to a roof or flood damage – Hurricane Harvey caused widespread flooding. Property insurance can help pay to fix or replace the portion of the building(s) affected and possibly compensate you for loss of rental income resulting from the damage.

Property insurance can also include coverage for earthquakes, debris removal, and vandalism repair, and many other things. Reach out to your broker if you have questions about your coverage.

About Kim Stallings, MBA

Kim is the proud owner and an agent at Heritage Risk Advisors.

Kim is an REI guru who travels all over giving public educational presentations on property insurance and real estate investing, and she loves it.

Contact Kim today with any questions you may have

Phone
940-367-9740

Email
kim@heritageriskadvisors.com

Website
HeritageRiskAdvisors.com

Facebook
Facebook.com/HeritageRisk

LinkedIn
LinkedIn.com/company/Heritage-Risk-Advisors

Instagram
Instagram.com/HeritageRisk.com

Twitter
Twitter.com/HeritageRisk

Chapter 17 – Lisa Hylton: Passive Investing in Syndications

Lisa Hylton is an account and a controller for private equality real estate funds. She is currently building a syndication business specifically focused on multifamily and apartments to provide opportunities for those with extremely demanding jobs who want to invest in real estate and have no desire to be a landlord.

Lisa shares the pros and cons of passively investing in real estate.

Cons of Investing as a Passive Investor

If you choose to take the syndication passive investor route, be aware of some of the potential cons:

1. You have no control of the business plan for the property or when the property is sold.

2. You are leveraging the time and expertise of someone else, so you want to make sure that you pick the right people with whom to invest.

3. Some people believe "passive" means they don't need to do any work.

Make sure that you even though you're investing passively, you spend time learning about and understanding the asset class for the investment.

You work hard for your money, so be a good steward of it and put it into the right markets and right asset classes with the right operators.

Typically, doing your due diligence correctly, becoming a sophisticated investor who's knowledgeable about the people and the asset class, that reduces or eliminate some risk.

PROS OF INVESTING AS A PASSIVE INVESTOR

As a controller of funds that invest in real estate, Lisa's job is extremely demanding and requires long hours. So, passively investing is an excellent option for people who don't have a lot of time to focus on remodeling an asset in another state.

Some advantages of becoming a passive investor are as follows:

1. You can leverage the time and experience of people who are dedicated full-time to do this work. There are many good operators who will provide details and reports to keep you informed. You're able to free up your time, because now your money is out there working for you and you're not trading time for money.

2. As a passive investor, you start to really understand asset classes like apartments, mobile home parks, and industrial properties. Then, you are better able to determine in which markets and assets to invest.

3. You build relationships with operators and can start to diversify your portfolio by investing in different real estate asset classes.

4. Cost segregation studies are performed on the properties so you're not paying any taxes on operating distributions or increasing your gross income.

5. You can use your money to change a community and provide jobs for others while making money.

WHAT ARE THE TAX ADVANTAGES AS A PASSIVE INVESTOR?

The primary tax advantage occurs when the operator does a cost segregation study. This allows them to accelerate the depreciation expense on certain aspects of the property in three to five. So, operating distributions from that property are offset by these paper expenses and investors don't pay any taxes on all the operating income received.

For example, an 8%, pref on a $100K investment results in about $8,000 coming to you for that year. If the cost segregation study has a loss, you could end with an actual loss. As a result, you won't pay any taxes on that $8,000 until the property is sold.

The real estate tax code is created in a way to incentivize people to build businesses and invest, provide housing for others, and create jobs. And that's amazing.

CHOOSING THE RIGHT TEAM

Networking and education are key to finding the right team. Listen to podcasts with operators and sponsors. Get to know people by visiting their websites and reading their blogs and articles.

Attend meetups and join groups with other passive investors and ask members, Hey, have you invested with this person before? What has been your experience?

Don't be afraid to ask operators about their track record. Visit some of their properties if you live close by. If you're going to invest $50K-$100K+, then spending $200-$400 to travel to view a property isn't too much to invest.

Take your time to get to know the sponsor. When someone brings you a deal, find out who the operator will be and who will be physically managing this deal day in day out so you can get to know them. Do your due diligence and learn about their track record. Remember:

You make money when you buy the asset, but you keep your money when you manage the asset properly.

QUESTIONS TO ASK A POTENTIAL TEAM

It would be really beneficial when someone presents a deal to you that they would also show their current deals, the role they're playing on these deals, who's managing the day-to-day, and underwriting versus actual. Also, what is the current status of their existing deals?

It would be great to see a portfolio of all their deals, how they're performing, and what investors on those deals are experiencing in terms of returns. Share the struggles they've had because let's face it, COVID has been challenging for everyone. But show how they are dealing with it and overcoming it.

If you're dealing with an investor who doesn't come from that background, they probably don't know to ask these questions.

More Information

To learn more about Lisa and passive investing, visit LisaHylton.com to download her seven-day Passive Investing Made Easy series.

About Lisa Hylton

Lisa Hylton is a real estate investor, syndicator, and a CPA with approximately 15 years of experience in the financial services industry. Lisa started out with a Big 4 accounting firm auditing billion-dollar funds across private equity, venture capital, mutual and hedge funds in the Cayman Islands, Boston, and Los Angeles. Lisa currently works as a controller on private equity real estate funds while investing passively and actively in primarily commercial real estate investments such as large multifamily apartment buildings.

Lisa's first exposure to real estate started with a 2 bedroom, 2 bathroom townhouse in the Cayman Islands that she bought in her early 20s. This first investment taught Lisa many lessons, primarily the importance of investing for cash flow and how to run the numbers on a property to assess whether it will be an investment with a high likelihood of cash flowing. Fast forward 10 plus years, Lisa's preferred way to invest in real estate is through passive and active syndications. To date, Lisa has invested in two syndications as a limited partner totaling 850 units in the Atlanta MSA and one sub-syndication raising 500K with my team of fellow Real Estate Investor Goddesses.

Lisa is also the host of the Level Up REI podcast which airs on Tuesdays and have featured series on the different ways people can play in real estate, Successful Black Men Investing in real estate, The Successful Feminine Real estate Business Owners, and the Black Entrepreneurs Leveling Up Series!

Originally from the Cayman Islands, Lisa currently resides in Los Angeles and enjoys dancing argentine tango, salsa, paddle boarding, yoga, hiking, reggae and soca music and traveling.

CONTACT LISA

Website
www.lisahylton.com

Instagram
@lisahyl
@thelevelupREI

Facebook
Facebook.com/Lisa.Hylton.92

The Level Up REI Podcast Group
Facebook.com/groups/787834775013292/

LinkedIn
LinkedIn.com/in/Lisa-Hylton-0b992815/

Twitter
Twitter.com/LisaHylton16

Chapter 18 – Karolina DiMario: Apartment Underwriter Toolset

Karolina DiMario came to the United States from Sweden when she was 18 years old to attend college. After earning her degree in Business Economics, she accepted a position in the telecom industry.

In 2012, she started investing in rentals to build wealth before getting involved in multifamily. Now, she underwrites for multiple investment groups.

Getting Started

Karolina started in real estate through "house hacking." She bought a duplex and lived in the smaller unit while renting out the other unit. Making sacrifices or being uncomfortable now will allow her to be live more comfortable later.

She continues to drive an old car, opting to invest that money in other single-family homes or multifamily properties.

You have to live like nobody else to live like nobody else later.

Biggest Lesson

In 2015, Karolina decided to buy her second duplex to live in one unit and have paying tenants in the other unit. After waiting for something in her price range to come on the market, she rushed to put in an offer despite the warning signs and red flags everywhere. The listing agent was rude and unhelpful. She was intimidated of the current tenant and there were issues every step of the way in the loan process.

Still, she didn't listen to her gut and continued moving forward. Finally, 2-3 days before closing escrow, the listing agent told her the garage exemption application was denied, and one unit would have to be converted back to a garage. At that point, she chose to cancel and not move forward with the deal.

A week later, another duplex came on the market in a much better area with great tenants. The listing agent was amazing, and Karolina learned a lot from him during the process.

As a woman, trust your gut feeling and have faith that something better is just around the corner.

UNDERWRITING

Underwriting describes collecting, organizing, and analyzing financial information and then using it to create projections of incomes, expenses, and investor returns.

UNDERWRITING A PROPERTY

When you begin to analyze a property, first verify that the offer price makes sense. Look at both price per unit and cap rates. If it's listed at a 4% cap rate, but the market is 6% cap rate, you know there is a discrepancy somewhere.

Next, search for reviews about the property to learn what the tenants are saying. You can learn a lot about the property and management by reading reviews. A significant crime history or an onsite shooting will make it difficult to get a loan. So, it might be best to pass at that point.

Then, do a quick Google Map search to see the surrounding area and businesses. Strip clubs or factories nearby would be undesirable. If there's a Home Depot, Lowe's, or Starbucks in the area, that's usually a good indicator it's a good location because these companies do a lot of market research before they put a store somewhere.

T12

After doing an initial analysis of the property, request the T12 (trailing 12 months of income and expenses) from the current owner.

Start by doing a stick test. For example, sum the months up to ensure the totals are correct and only includes 12 months' data.

Continue skimming through the report looking for anomalies and make detailed notes of your findings. For example, a lot of bad debt and late fee income indicates that tenants are not paying their rents on time.

Another red flag would be missing amounts for one month, which may cause total expenses to be artificially understated.

Using the Underwriting Tool

Input all of the T12 information into the system you are using, including Gross potential rent, vacancies, loss to lease, other income, and expenses broken down into each expense category.

Using the T12 numbers as a guide along with expected expenses of a stabilized property of a similar size, project what your income and expenses will be the first year. Make sure to use the knowledge of the analysis of the T12, rent roll, and property research accordingly. For example, if rents include utilities and the T12 was from 70% occupancy, then utilities will grow accordingly as occupancy increases. If many reviews mention pest issues, you will need to project an increase in contract services to pay for regular pest control services.

Management fees and Insurance costs will vary depending on property type, size, and location. Always get a quote on these.

Projecting Real Estate Taxes requires you to fully understand millage rates, assessment ratio, and reassessment cadency. This varies depending on state and location.

Rent Rolls

Review the rent rolls to look for artificially inflated occupancy rates such as large number of new leases, a lot of leases set to expire soon, or several leases for people with the same last name.

The rent roll will tell you the property's current occupancy. You need at least 90% occupancy for 90 days to get agency debt. If the occupancy is below 90%, you may need to do a bridge loan with a higher interest rate.

Then, calculate the average current rent per floor plan and use this with your rental comp analysis to determine current market rents.

RENTAL COMP ANALYSIS

This is one of the most important areas of underwriting. You can get your comparable information from commercial real estate information companies like costar. If you don't have access to those, you can visit sites like apartments.com and find nearby comparable properties in the area with a similar age and amenities. Make a note of the rents, the unit size, and the amenities available. Visit or call the properties to confirm that the rates that you found are correct. Make note of material differences, such as utilities included and better amenities.

Next, do the same but for properties that are renovated to help you determine how much you would be able to get in rents if you do any renovations.

Before deciding if you want to renovate, see if it makes sense financially. Estimate the cost to renovate each floor plan and then determine the number of months it would take to pay for the renovation costs using the renovation premium. A good guideline is for it to be no more than 3-4 years.

One strategy is to renovate only half of the units and then leave some meat on the bone for the next investor for an easier sale.

RENT GROWTH

This is an area where it is smart to estimate less than current rent growth. Even if the property is in a really hot market with rents going up by 7% every year, you probably still want to use a lower, more conservative number. Stay around the rate of inflation of 2% and even less in uncertain times.

EXIT STRATEGY

When analyzing a project, always consider your exit strategy and when you plan to sell the deal. Be conservative when estimating exit cap rates and assume they will be higher in the future. You always want to check the projected exit sales price per unit and make sure it aligns with nearby sales comps.

ADVANCED UNDERWRITING SPREADSHEET

There are several underwriting software programs and spreadsheets you can use to analyze a multifamily deal. After thousands of hours spent underwriting, Karolina developed an Advanced Underwriting Excel spreadsheet that is now available for purchase. It is an excellent resource for the beginner underwriter or experienced underwriter who needs a more flexible tool to take their underwriting to the next level.

Some key benefits to using this tool are:

- Accurately analyze any multifamily deal and investor returns

- Ability to quickly compare different business plans to determine which brings the best returns for your investors

- Ability to compare a loan assumption versus fresh debt scenario

- Detailed worksheets for a thorough rental comp analysis

- Incorporate renovations per year into your analysis

- Free updates of new versions

For more information about the Advanced Underwriting Spreadsheet, visit

TheApartmentQueen.com/Resources/Advanced-Underwriting-Spreadsheet

ABOUT KAROLINA DIMARIO

Karolina holds a B.S. in Business Economics from California State University, Long Beach. She has been at FreeConferenceCall.com since 2010 and works as the Director of Business Analytics. Karolina became an active real estate investor in 2012 and is personally managing her own portfolio of rentals in Southern California and Ohio. Analytical in nature, she enjoys analyzing multifamily properties and finding ways to improve the efficiency of the operations to maximize investor returns. She has been professionally underwriting multifamily deals since 2019.

To learn more about the underwriting spreadsheet developed by Karolina, you can contact her on her website.

Website
https://sveaventures.com

CHAPTER 19 – KATHY FETTKE: THE REAL WEALTH SHOW

After interviewing dozens of real estate millionaires on the *Real Wealth Show*, Kathy discovered some of their best strategies for creating passive income streams. She and her husband took their advice and purchased numerous cash-flowing investment properties. They have since learned the highs and lows of investing that can only come from hands-on experience.

Kathy is an active real estate investor, licensed real estate agent, and former mortgage broker. She shares how she specializes in helping people build multi-million dollar real estate portfolios that generate passive monthly cash flow for life.

GETTING STARTED

Like many entrepreneurs, Kathy considers herself unemployable. As a natural entrepreneur, she prefers to work for herself. The day she got a dirty look for arriving five minutes late to work because her kids needed extra help that morning, she decided she would never again allow anyone to control her time.

Kathy learned very young that her time was valuable and limited, and therefore, she wanted to spend it doing only the things she wanted to do. She found a job working in the news that she enjoyed. She also ran a successful modeling and acting business. After marrying her soul mate, Rich Fettke, and having two kids, she wanted to spend her time raising her children. She had a part-time job working from home, but it wasn't much.

In 2002, Rich was at the top of his game. He was a successful business coach and had recently written a book called "Extreme Success." When he returned from traveling around the world for his book tour, he went to the doctor to have an unusual freckle checked.

The doctors determined it was a fast-growing melanoma and thought it had spread to his liver. They told Rich he had six months to live. This was a huge shock, especially since he had always been an athlete, jumping out of airplanes, skiing steep mountains, and surfing big hurricane waves. Dying from skin cancer was not in the plan.

The good news is that Rich is healthy today, and the doctor was wrong. A surgeon cut the melanoma out, and Rich now gets tested regularly. But the experience forced Kathy to figure out their finances, in case the doctor was right.

Kathy became obsessed with learning how to create income from home to continue being a stay-at-home mom.

At the time, she was hosting a weekly radio show in San Francisco. She changed the show's topic to her new focus: *how to create passive income while being a stay-at-home mom.*

She started interviewing people who understood cash flow, asking what they did and how they did it. And it came down to two things: people who started a business or people who invested in real estate.

Creating a sustainable business was not new to Kathy but acquiring assets that created cash flow was a new concept. Interviewing people who were half her age and already retired gave Kathy the confidence to do it.

RAISING CAPITAL

At the time, Kathy was in a desperate position due to her husband's illness. Being a stay-at-home mom for years, she forgot what it was like out in the business world. But she did have her little radio show and learned from her guests that investing in real estate involved taking money you already have and investing it for the long-term.

But what about someone who doesn't have any money and needs to make money fast? Many investors start as wholesalers so they can flip a deal, make a chunk of money, and invest it in long-term real estate.

Kathy wondered how she could make a chunk of money without flipping houses, which she thought would be difficult with small children. She did have her radio show, which was an asset she could leverage. The obvious way that anyone makes money in radio is by selling advertising. She started calling people and asking them to advertise on the show.

After several "no" responses, she knew her next offer had to be irresistible. She opened the phone book and called a mortgage broker because, at the time, they were doing a lot of radio advertising.

Kathy asked, "How would you like to be the co-host of my radio show? I am looking for an expert. In exchange for your sponsorship/ partnership, you will become more widely known in our community." He said, "Tell me more. This is exactly what I've been looking for."

That was an excellent lesson. Focus on what others need and how you can help provide it. Then it's not a sale, but rather a service, a benefit.

The mortgage broker became a regular on the show and eventually a co-host. To keep the show interesting, they sought out people who were doing really cool things with mortgages, like flipping homes and BRRRR (Buy, Rehab, Rent, Refinance, Repeat).

Kathy and her audience soon learned that almost anyone could get a bank loan to finance their real estate deal.

The show became a huge success, and the mortgage broker's phone rang off the hook with people who wanted financing. He had so much new business that he encouraged Kathy to get her real estate license and become a mortgage broker to take some of the new clients.

STARTING HER BUSINESS

Kathy instantly became a very busy mortgage broker, and her financial worries were soon gone. She also discovered that many of her clients were coming to her not just for mortgages but also for financial advice. They didn't know what to do with their money.

Once she realized there was an incredible need for financial advice to build wealth from someone other than a typical financial planner, the business focus changed to help people find alternative investments to the stock market.

Although Kathy didn't know much about finances then, her co-host stepped in to mentor her. All of a sudden, she had too much business and too many people to help.

Instead of hiring someone to absorb some of the workload, Kathy took on a business partner who seemed to know what he was doing because he had a business degree.

LESSONS LEARNED

At the time, Kathy didn't think she could afford an employee, so she chose a partner instead. She didn't realize that he should have to buy into the company. He came in with no money and immediately started changing how things were done, despite his lack of experience. Kathy eventually had to buy him out of the partnership.

The buyout wasn't a huge expense, but it was a great lesson for Kathy early on to hire employees and be careful about bringing on partners. The first employees should be experts at things you are not good at or don't enjoy. For Kathy, it was definitely the bookkeeping and logistical details. She hired an experienced bookkeeper, an office manager, and a salesperson.

As things continued to grow rapidly, Kathy's husband joined the company and became her "chief support guy". He put up the website and created business systems, and together, they were able to grow the company.

As their company grew, Kathy learned another valuable lesson- the importance of clear communication and specific employee roles. It can really strain relationships if you don't have clear agreements in writing. Now, she only hires the best person for the job, no matter what they charge, because it frees up her time to focus on what she does best.

BIGGEST WIN

Kathy attributes much of her success to creating a platform where she could interview people smarter than her with 20, 30, or 40 years' experience. She interviewed Robert Kiyosaki on *The Real Wealth Show,* learned what he was doing, and as a result, guided people in the right direction in 2005.

He told her that cash flow was king, and he was selling all of his high-priced California properties and 1031 exchanging into cash flow properties in Dallas, TX. This seems like an obvious move today, but back then, people thought she was nuts. They didn't think anything special was happening in Texas, but that's because they weren't following demographics.

Kathy and Rich ended up buying seven homes in the Dallas area, and helped thousands of other people do the same. Those who sold their California homes at the peak of the market in 2005 and exchanged them for little cash flow homes in Texas, tripled and even quadrupled their cash flow in that one move. Since then, most have also tripled or quadrupled their equity and never felt the recession.

Kathy's real estate investment group, Real Wealth Network, now has over 54,000 members. Her podcast, *The Real Wealth Show*, has over 5 million downloads and continues to feature guests with varying experiences to guide listeners in the right direction.

CONTACT KATHY FETTKE

If you have any questions about alternative investments, you can visit Kathy's website at www.RealWealthNetwork.com/About/Kathy-Fettke.

From there, you can join her Real Wealth network, which is free and includes education and guidance to help investors make good decisions and start a cash-flowing portfolio. She also has 18 teams in the nation's top real estate markets who find, renovate, and manage rental properties for investors.

You can listen to *The Real Wealth Show: Real Estate Investing Podcast* for insights on creating passive income through real estate and avoiding costly mistakes. Learn how to build a portfolio outside the stock market with buy-and-hold strategies, single-family rentals, multifamily properties, syndicated deals, self-directed IRAs and 401ks, the highly-revered 1031 exchange, private money lending, creative financing, and much more!

Chapter 20 – Shannon Shackerley-Bennett: Hotel Developer and CEO

In addition to multifamily properties, investors can invest in commercial properties in the hospitality sector. Hotels can be very lucrative for investors but are the most susceptible to economic swings.

Shannon Shackerley-Bennett, owner and founder of North Star Hotel Development, shares her experience with hotel development projects.

Hotel Development Properties

North Star Hotel Development is a pre-construction developer that offers professional services to enable the capital raise, acquisition, and entitlement for multifamily and branded hotels, plus syndication of deals for existing hospitality and multifamily investments across the nation.

The initial focus is capital raise to purchase property, then proposing a new project to a city that would be built that land (hospitality projects and hotels). Once the city approves the project, they typically sell the land to a builder. It's a bit like flipping a home, but there are a lot more rooms.

Investing in Hospitality

Hospitality is unique because the land is an appreciable asset that appreciates over time and doesn't generate any income. So, the asset manager needs to monetize that land.

Then, a business, such as a hotel, sits on top of that land.

The same person does not always own the land and the business. About 30% of hotels are built on ground leases, which creates a line-item and affects cash flow.

Cash-flow Investments

Many of the investments North Star Hotel Development participates in don't flow cash very quickly but have a return time that many investors view as short-term. When acquiring a property, it takes about a year to entitle it and get approvals for the new project.

For example, North Star recently acquired some land in San Jose for $6.5 million. The entitlement costs will be about $1 million, resulting in a total $7.5 million sunk into this project.

None of the investors who came into this project a year ago have seen any cash flow. There's no income, only expenses. As we come to approvals, almost a year later, this becomes a very attractive piece of land for builders who want to land bank to sell to a hotel owner/operator eventually, and that's who will ultimately purchase this property. The expected appraisal should come in between $9.5 and $10 million, which is reduced because of where the hospitality industry is today due to COVID and market pricing.

Even during COVID, there were offers. At that point, the investors were told an offer of $9.8 million could be accepted now. But holding the land and waiting 12 months could potentially result in an offer of $13 million.

> Land Bank: Buying and holding a property knowing that it will appreciate and sold for profit.

The investors in that project are forecasting between 22 to 25% annualized returns, which is pretty healthy. But there's no cash flow, monthly or quarterly distribution while they wait for that return.

On the flip side, an investor can invest in a property that will be purchased for $4 million with an estimated 6% pref return quarterly.

> A pref is a preferred return. An investor who agrees to a pref return will get a predetermined amount before anyone else gets funds from the deal.

One scenario is very unknown with a high degree of risk when entitling property and working with public and city and architects or vendor teams that may or may not perform. And even after you build it, you may not have a buyer. Investors must be aware of all risks and ask the person presenting the offering, "What is your exit strategy?"

This is no different than flipping a house. You can pretty it up and add value, but if you don't have a buyer, you won't have profits.

Understand what kind of investor you are. Are you willing to take that risk? As a passive investor, can you sit by and you watch other make decisions without jumping in and saying, "Hey, actually, I think that should be Hilton, not Hyatt." Those decisions are made by the management team, not by passive investors.

PRIVATE PLACEMENT MEMORANDUM (PPM)

Every offering that North Star Hotel Development includes a PPM, which contains key information about the offering. This will be a dense document that should include the following information:

- Operating agreement for the company in which you are investing

- The pro forma showing the future value

- The cost of the project

- Use of funds (What are they going to use the funds for?)

- Ways in which you can hold them accountable to using those funds

For some deals, companies may use a subscription model. Investors purchase shares in the company, creating a limited partnership that does not grant any decision-making rights. A subscription agreement will outline what they're investing in, how many shares they're buying, the current value, and the expected return. However, investors must be aware that there's no guarantee of a return, so the following is also included in the PPM:

- Management risks

- Project risks

- Market risks

- COVID risks

- Any other potential risks

By the time you finish reading that, if you still feel that you want to take the risk, review the subscription document that subscribes you to the shares. In that document, you will see your preferred rate of return for taking the risk.

If the management of the offering has misunderstood the market and overpriced or overestimated the exit value, there won't be enough funds to return money back to you at that pref rate. So, even if the subscription agreement states you have a pref rate of 6%, if there are insufficient profits in that project to return 6%, you're not going to see it.

What's the guarantee? There is no guarantee. These are high-risk investments.

RETURN ON INVESTMENT

Every deal is structured differently, and most often have at least five partners. We generally offer a 70/30 split, and we prefer equity over offering a pref. We give up a lot more money, but it's easier to manage expectations.

In a 70/30 split, 30% will be held for the company and 70% goes to the passive investors. Typically, but not always, payouts are proportional based on the percentage of shares purchased.

If your company has 100 shares and someone purchases one share, that person owns 1%. So, when you distribute the profits, that person will get 1% of the 70%.

Some interesting math flows through to show an effective percentage overall in the company, primarily for tax purposes. Investors can estimate their based on an assumed sales value or net operating income.

EXIT STRATEGIES

Like in multifamily investing, investors in the hospitality sector should always question the exit strategy for a project.

For example, due to COVID, buyers may be reluctant to purchase because lenders are uncertain about the industry's future, so projects that began pre-COVID may not have profits. And that's a difficult conversation to have with investors. But you can make it easier by bringing them along in the journey. Nobody wants to get a phone call after two years saying, "Hey, this didn't work out the way I thought we were going to exit." Passive investors can stay informed through weekly meetings and monthly reports. They don't have to attend the meetings or read the reports, but the option is available.

North Star has a very solid pool of buyers, over 200 that are pre-qualified—not just proof of funds, either. These individuals have the credentials, have been certified by the brands to operate these assets, and are actively seeking sites to expand their business.

In March 2020, when COVID started to really show itself, North Star was actively marketing a project they were ready to sell. Buyers started going really quiet. Some started to say, "Hey, I'm going to hold my cash because I don't know what's going to happen. I need to be able to meet my current obligations before I can start a new project."

Then, it started to change to, "Hey, I might be able to pick up distressed assets that I could run and operate for less than it will cost me to build this new one."

So, we began having weekly conversations with the investors and identified seven different contingency plans.

- Can I get a JV partner?
- Can I get a JV partner who will take out my investors?
- Can I get a JV partner that will cover my debt servicing?
- Can I move?
- Can I get my investors to pitch in more and take out debt servicing so that I can get more time to sell?
- Do we land bank?
- Do we sell at a loss?

While you're meeting with investors, you should also be having conversations with your lender and making sure that you can get extensions to pay your debt servicing. Look at any and all options These are all viable options, but some of them are not desirable.

Remember when you're having these conversations that your investors are really in a difficult situation because they may feel that they don't have a say, and, ultimately, the decisions are made by management. However, including them in the journey, listening to their concerns, and addressing those concerns as best as one can create a great deal of understanding and maybe even goodwill. Investors may come up with other solutions that the management team may not have ever considered. Some suggest selling stocks, getting a loan on their home, or taking another mortgage – they may be prepared to invest more.

Another option is to find a joint venture partner with the goal to exit investors whole and healthy. This means creating a situation that preserves capital so that returns are still possible. Sometimes, the management team ultimately leaves equity in the deal and becomes unintended owners of an asset to meet the objectives.

You need to manage your work and be creative in finding solutions. You can't throw your arms up in the air and walk away. Figure out *one way* that you can make it happen.

It's also important that you have a strong network of people to help you pivot, such as an experienced general counsel and tax CPA.

If you're an investor in a project, ask that company:

- Who are your resources?

- Who do you ask for help?

- Who's in your mentorship team?

- Who are your advisors?

If they don't have any, they're limiting their perspective.

INSURANCE

Often, project managers will feel more comfortable moving forward with a project if they are insured. Insurance in the hospitality and development industries is really complex. It's important that you speak to an advisor to help you select insurance for each individual project.

Also, be aware that your lender may have specific requirements about the amount and type of insurance policy you carry beyond hazard insurance. Policies can vary depending on if there is a vacant lot or a vacant building on the property.

Some providers won't insure certain types of assets. You need to understand who to go to in the industry that will perform the way you expect so that your interpretation of the policy matches theirs and meets the lender's requirements.

USING HARD MONEY FOR HOSPITALITY PROPERTIES

Conventional loans are not typically used to finance hospitality projects. Often this is because it takes less time to work with a private lender who tends to be more open to financing projects that start with bare land or a non-income producing property. Sometimes, the property doesn't appraise high enough, or the lender doesn't see the future value. There's no accounting for that future value, making it a hard sell for conventional banks.

You need to find several sources for investors. Be very careful when going into these deals and ensure you can live by the terms of the deal.

If investors are offered 20-25% annualized returns for purchasing shares in the company, and a hard money loan is 10%, maximize as much private money as you can when you're confident that there is sufficient lift in the project value. You don't need to be greedy, but you need to ensure you have a successful project.

When looking at a term sheet, note how you feel about the initial interaction with this person.

- What do their documents look like?
- What does the application request be provided?
- Are they a complete disaster organizationally?
- Are they professional?

If you run into problems later, you want to have a professional discussion with a professional.

Then, look at the **terms**.

- Will I have enough time?

- Is an extension available to me?

- Do I have to pay for an extension?

- Do I have to apply for an extension?

- Is an extension automatic?

- Is there a balloon payment?

- Can I raise funds to manage a balloon payment if it happens?

- Will the payments be collected by a servicing company or the lender themselves?

- Will I be Venmo-ing cash and trying to do it in chunks?

- Am I writing one check to send to a servicer?

These are the things to look for when evaluating the opportunities to leverage hard money.

HOSPITALITY AND CASH FLOW

There are so many different cash-flowing assets for investors. What you choose to invest in depends on the market. If you have a market that needs mobile homes, you may chase mobile homes, especially if that intrigues you.

Shannon Shackerley-Bennett fell into hospitality, and she loves it. Being a developer increases her depth of involvement with the industry, which allowed her to become an expert. She is often invited to speak at conferences and is a continual lifelong learner.

Although she is brand agnostic – meaning she is not a franchisee of any brand, she is familiar with all of them. She relies on her good relationships with the top 10 brands in the United States, plus one in Canada, and another in Europe that wants to expand into America.

In addition, she belongs to associations and sponsors activities where owner/operators will be. She attends legislative summits to advocate because she understands important issues in the industry and is proud to represent the industry and offer a public voice.

So, why hotels? Part of it is a passion for and a belief in an industry that demonstrates profitability. For any businessperson, something that is profitable is attractive. Combine that with a love for travel that brings enjoyable new experiences, and it's hard to beat a career as a hotel developer. Finding something you love to do that makes a profit is a beautiful combination.

ABOUT SHANNON SHACKERLEY-BENNETT

Shannon Shackerley-Bennett, BA, PMP, is the sole owner of North Star Hotel Development, LLC, a sister company to North Star Development. She is an Active Managing Member and serves as the Chief Executive Officer for both companies.

As a dynamic leader, she creates results through strong communication, organizational, and professional abilities. More than 25 years of progressively responsible positions with corporate, new business, and start-up teams have given Shackerley-Bennett the practical knowledge and leadership skills to manage risk and solve complex challenges.

Previously, Shannon was the Chief Operating Officer of a real estate development firm. There, she was responsible for the strategic direction and daily operation of a company overseeing $90M+ of commercial real estate holdings with over a million sq feet of build-out potential in the Silicon Valley.

In May 2019, she was recognized and honored at the BisNow's Bay Area Power Women event as one of 30 "Dynamic women in commercial real estate for their outstanding achievements in the office, their industry, and our communities." Most months, Shannon delivers presentation material or participates in interviews about her experiences and expertise in the real estate and land development sectors.

With 15+ years as an Owner and Property Manager of income-producing properties, recent syndication experience, and a long corporate career, Shannon is well-positioned for structuring new business ventures and partnerships.

Contact Shannon

Website
NorthstarDevGroup.com/

LinkedIn
LinkedIn.com/in/ShannonShackerleyBennett/

The
Apartment
Queen

We are looking for more investors like you.

Please complete The Apartment Queen™
Investor Questionnaire to be added to
our list for events and deals:
https://form.jotform.com/200207883604451

Our ideal investor is typically one of these following
Ultimate passive investors:
WOMEN with 1031 Exchange over $400K
High Net Worth Individuals
Doctors
Dentists
Engineers
Individual with 10 Years' Experience at a Company
Real Estate Brokers/Agents
Female Athletes
Aggie Women
Women CEO, Founder
Socialites
Duchess/Heiress
Individuals with Pension Funds
Endowments
Women-owned Family Offices
Those with Funds Who Support the Social Initiative
to Teach Financial Literacy to Women
Angel Investors Supporting Women

CHAPTER 21 – DAWN WAYE: PROPERTY MANAGEMENT

Dawn Waye is the President of City Gate Property Group, a property management group that provides excellent services to its residents and clients. Working in property management since having a part-time receptionist job at a property management company while attending nursing school, Dawn still loves it years later.

GETTING STARTED

After joining Knightvest Management as the Vice President of Operations, Dawn was given the opportunity to purchase a third-party business and founded City Gate Property Group. Knightvest Management owned several assets, and when they would sell those, buyers would often ask if Knightvest would continue the property management.

After building up 12 to 15 assets, they decided third-party management diluted their focus on owned assets.

Dawn knew she would someday have her own management company, but on a smaller scale, catering to smaller assets. After adjusting to the shock of jumping into owning a third-party management company, she started very small, reducing the number of units from 1200 to 850. Then, the company began to gain steam and never looked back, growing to over 17,000 units and 85 to 90 properties.

The excitement of having her own business wasn't there from the very beginning; instead, she experienced fright. But she kept at it, working one day at a time while learning everything about every position in the business. The company now has 450 employees, and Dawn could probably jump in to help with any task. She's touched and felt everything from setting up the bank accounts, processing asset management fees, and putting a financial together. A lot happens behind the scenes that people never see, so many are surprised when they venture out on their own at how tough it can be.

When first starting with few employees, understand that everyone will be wearing multiple hats. City Group Property Management now has five people who handle the marketing and two others to do training, and they cross-train employees.

Although they're not trainers, the members of the support department are experts at what they do, so they can conduct training as well.

The truth is, it's not all pretty and sparkly. Be willing to take on challenges and accept that you won't always know the answer. Continue pressing forward and learning. You may fail, but you'll learn something along the way—that's the reality right of being an entrepreneur. Consider finding a mentor or someone willing to share their experience and walk through the process with you.

THE BIGGEST LESSON

For Dawn, her biggest lesson as a business owner has been accepting that she's not perfect and is going to make mistakes. She understands that when she or an employee has done something that might cause a problem, she needs to address it right away.

She will confront or communicate with a client sooner rather than later to prevent anxiousness from building up inside of her. She removes all emotion from the situation, which can be difficult, especially if you're a woman. There's an answer for anything and everything. You just have to find the answer and develop a viable solution. Being honest, truthful, and sincere with people often diffuses an uncomfortable situation.

Many people fear rejection or having someone yell at them, but the best thing to do is move forward and fix any mistakes as quickly as possible.

If you think somebody is upset with you, ask them, "Are you upset with me?" Put to rest any negative thoughts so that you can move on.

As long as you aren't doing anything unethical, immoral, or illegal, you can come at any situation with the best resources you have. If you don't have the answer, humble yourself and find someone who does or work with others to figure it out together.

THE BIGGEST WIN

For Dawn, her biggest win comes from the feeling she gets from taking the jump and opening her business without being afraid. She didn't look back, and the possibility of failing never crossed her mind. Her biggest concern was what would happen when the company got so big that all of her resources were over-extended.

If you're afraid, do it afraid.

When your business starts growing, align yourself with a partner who is smarter than you and whose education and experience complement yours. Dawn's business partner has a level of education and expertise different than hers, and they work great together.

City Gate Property Group hires the best and the brightest. They have an amazing CFO, controller, and back-office staff. Surround yourself with smart people who know something that you don't, and the missing pieces will come together.

You don't have to know everything about each position in your business. It can be intimidating when a partner or employee is more knowledgeable in one area but have faith every step of the way, and you will see that you learn from each other. Understanding who you are as a person and what value you bring. Communicating openly with your employees and clients and be willing to face situations head-on will ensure your success.

PROPERTY MANAGEMENT BEST PRACTICES

When looking at a property, consider the following (not necessarily in this order):

1. People

2. Price

3. Promotion

4. Product

Having the right people doing the right job with the right attitude transcends any business. On any level, if you have the wrong people to do the tasks, you will be fighting an uphill battle.

PEOPLE

Sometimes we find our greatness in working with people that are diverse from us, which opens up the playing field. Working with only people in your lane will limit your business. Broaden your horizons and work with every type of personality.

People want to work at City Gate Property Group because they know who we are and what our heart, mind, and philosophy are. Always look for people who have that X factor and are really passionate about what they do. If you're not passionate about accounting and numbers, find someone who is. Life's too short to spend it miserable. Have a reason to get up in the morning and be excited about what you're doing, or else life's a void,

Nothing changes until you change it. Find people who don't need constant praise or words of encouragement; they can generate that from within themselves.

PRICE, PROMOTION, AND PRODUCT

The price, promotion, and product are specific to a property. Making sure you have the right product can transcend whether you're looking at an apartment or you're looking at marketing for your company.

Does your product look nice? Does it have curb appeal? Can a customer find what they need when they go to your website? You can apply much of what you learn in the multifamily real estate industry to other industries.

WHAT TO KNOW WHEN INTERVIEWING PROPERTY MANAGEMENT COMPANIES

Before you interview a property management company, prepare some information about your property and your business. What are your goals? Be sure the property management company knows your goals and where you want to be so they can make a plan to help you succeed.

Establish a relationship and build trust with each other. You're allowing this company to handle your multimillion-dollar baby, so trust is essential.

Key questions an investor should ask a property management company:

- What are your best practices?
- What do you do?
- Will you work towards our goal?
- Will you establish a plan?
- How quickly will you address a problem at the property?
- Will you notify us if there is a problem at the property?
- How often will you provide reports?

COMMUNICATIONS BETWEEN PROPERTY MANAGERS AND PROPERTY OWNERS

Typically, you can expect to have more communication than normal when a property manager first takes over your asset. After establishing that operations are running normally and trust is building, direct communications are less frequent. Clients can pull reports directly from the software system, allowing managers more time to walk vacant apartments, walk the property, and collaborate with the team to determine any needs.

A good property manager will let you know if you need to replace your boiler the day it goes down; you won't find out about it on your financials.

A good property management company exists to make you money, solve your problems, and let you sleep while they can't. They should do whatever it takes to make you comfortable and reassure you that your property is doing well, and you have nothing to worry about.

CONTACT DAWN

If you have any questions about City Gate Property Group or asset property management, reach out to Dawn at dwaye@CityGatePG.com, through her website at www.CityGatePropertyGroup.com, or via phone at 214-223-6090.

ABOUT DAWN WAYE

With over 20 plus years in the multifamily industry, Dawn's experience is well-rounded and multi-faceted, built upon her passion for
marketing, training, asset management, business development, and
operation of all asset types. Dawn joined the real estate business at 18,
starting as a receptionist for Ferland Corporation in Rhode Island.
Shortly after, she was promoted to Executive Assistant to the Vice
President of Conventional Operations, broadening her experience in
appraisals and acquisitions. Her family's military duties moved her to
Florida, where she managed and operated the property management
division for a large family-owned firm.

Ms. Waye later joined a development and asset management firm
focused on tax credit and multi-use, high-rise new construction. Dawn
was hired as an Investment Manager at Pinnacle Properties to oversee
the renovation and lease-up of a mixed-use, historical tax credit development in downtown Dallas. After joining Knightvest Management as the
Vice President of Operations, she was afforded the opportunity to

purchase a third-party business and founded City Gate Property Group. Dawn holds a broker licenses in Texas, Oklahoma, Rhode Island, Arkansas and Florida, as wells as a national CPM Designation. As a leader in her industry, she provides our clients, vendors, and residents a voice at the local, state, and national level through legislative advocacy. Dawn has sat on panels representing the industry, and all of her colleagues embrace her entrepreneurial spirit.

Website
CityGatePropertyGroup.com

Chapter 22 – Karen Oeser, CFA: From Traditional to Alternative Investments

Karen Oeser is the principal of East Light Investments, a company that partners with passive investors to acquire value-add apartment buildings in the southeast. She often speaks to groups at large seminars because she loves sharing her knowledge on this topic and helping women in any way.

Karen shares how as a Chartered Financial Analyst (CFA) and a Certified Financial Education Instructor, she helps others move from traditional investments to alternative investments.

Getting Started

Karen has been in the investment business for about 25 years. When her children were small, she started a consulting firm. It was completely bootstrapped and financed using a home equity line. Her first successful flip piqued her interest in real estate after seeing how quickly it worked.

To fund her latest business, East Light investments, she cashed out of the stock market. With a background in traditional investing, she has been able to extract and apply the skills necessary to diversify her portfolio the right way.

Solo 401k

A Solo 401k plan is the same as a traditional 401k, but it is available specifically for owner-only businesses that do not employ full-time, non-owner W-2 employees.

You can use a Solo 401k as a traditional investment vehicle by self-directing it to investments you choose. Account holders have "checkbook control," which allows them to write a check to invest in any asset that is not disallowed under IRS regulations.

OTHER OPTIONS

Today, there are many more creative options available for investing than when Karen started in single-family homes. And right now, there couldn't be a better time to transition into multifamily. No matter where you are with your financial assets, there's a place for you in the real estate market.

BIGGEST CHALLENGES

One of the biggest hurdles when moving from traditional investing to multifamily investing is determining where to pull assets from to put into multifamily. The barriers to entry are very high, which can be limiting. But that's also a good thing because it presents opportunity from a supply and demand standpoint—if you know what you're doing.

Anyone just getting started in multifamily investing should get involved with a coaching program, not only for the educational aspects but to network with like-minded individuals. You will learn something about multifamily from everyone you meet while lowering the barrier of entry into the investing community.

OVERCOMING PERSONAL CHALLENGES

Karen can talk stocks and bonds all day, but she thought, "Who am I to talk about real estate? I don't know anything about it, other than I successfully flipped a few single-family homes." It's different moving from a $75,000 investment in a single-family house to a multi-million multifamily investment.

Becoming comfortable speaking the real estate language was one of the biggest hurdles for Karen to overcome. Shifting from finance to plumbing, EPA rules, and getting engineering documents together was challenging. However, she is now surrounded by a team of people who are thrilled to share their expertise, enabling her to quickly gain confidence.

SHIFTING FROM SINGLE-FAMILY TO MULTIFAMILY

Karen relies heavily on her team, especially when it comes to dealing with legal matters and contractors. Doing single-family flips, she found many contractors tried to take advantage at any opportunity. In multifamily, only a handful of companies are large enough to flip 20 units in two weeks at an effective price point. Because there are so few, they really care about their reputation. They don't play games and do a good job.

Another important distinction in the multifamily world that stood out to Karen is that everyone involved works together. When you attend conferences, you know the names. And if you don't, someone else who can vouch for them will. The bad eggs don't last very long.

Also, the charitable mindset of people in multifamily has really captured her heart. There's a lot of money to be made in this industry. You can't take it with you when you leave this world, but you can leave your mark in this world.

Your mess is your message. When you figure out how to fix it, then share that solution with others.

BIGGEST WIN

Karen's biggest win was joining a group called *Aspiring Women Achieving More* to find an accountability group after hearing about it at one of Rod Khleif's boot camps.

She was hesitant to go in front of these powerhouse women at first, fearing they would judge her. But she bravely took the leap and went from zero to 60 in three months by being humble and vulnerable and joining that group.

Any time you lay down your pride and ask for help, ask for advice, ask for what you want, you will receive more than you ever imagined in return. Karen was surprised at how quickly her new tribe was willing to support her through her challenges and celebrate in her victories.

Now, deals are flowing from Springdale, AK, to Greenville, South Carolina. So, networking and team building are essential to meeting people in other markets. Through these groups that she's joined, she's been able to find boots on the ground.

LEADERSHIP AND WOMEN IN MULTIFAMILY

A good leader can easily recognize the strengths of individuals in a group. Then, everyone on the team can stay in their lane, focusing on their strengths. When the team comes together, they can collaborate on what's been done and what needs to be done and find a solution to get it done. A leader can keep the teams moving forward individually and in groups.

Throw problems at the wall and see if which team members have a better solution. Take five minutes to make a phone call if you're unsure about something. Everybody having their own skill set is key to avoiding challenges.

Remember, you can learn a lot from others who possess a skill set that you do not have. Learning from each other takes your team to a higher level. The rising tide raises all ships

Karen enjoys working directly with people. Finding solutions for residents who may be ill or going through a challenging time allows you to make it work for everyone. You don't need to kick them out or allow them to take advantage of your business, but you can find middle ground. Be solution-focused and figure it out.

Be flexible and be open because the world isn't in a silo. Look for opportunities because that's where you'll find the victories and excitement.

When you have two pieces of information, you can find a third way to leverage that. Connect with somebody who understands multifamily and traditional investing.

About Karen Oeser

Karen is a passionate advocate for financial literacy. After managing multi-million portfolios across the globe for nearly 25 years, she launched "Financial Literacy for Her" to help women overcome their fear of money and empower them to build generational wealth. Women control over half the wealth in this country, yet most are afraid to discuss it and leave their potential fortunes to make pennies on the dollar after taxes and inflation. Karen specially designed "Financial Literacy for Her" as a safe place where women can be vulnerable and ask difficult questions without judgment. As part of the program, each client is partnered with a knowledgeable coach to create a diversified wealth plan to help them realize their dreams. Also, clients will be teamed up with other like-minded women to share in their journeys.

In her capacity as a pastor and Licensed Minister of Dance, Karen works with families who have loved ones struggling with drug addiction, mental illness, and incarceration. In her free time, she loves spending time with her teenage sons, being in the outdoors, traveling, and volunteering at her church.

Contact Karen Oeser

Be sure to visit Karen's website to download a free report, which details the 10 reasons she left the investment business and how it applies to multifamily, such as expenses, earnings, and how interest rates work for you. It's an excellent primer for anyone who wants to see how the two worlds work together.

Website
EastLightInvest.com

Email
Karen@EastLightInvest.com

Phone
864-551-1820

Chapter 23 – Leka Devatha: Making Millions with Small Multifamily

Leka Devatha began her love affair with real estate in 2014. She started as an investor doing single-family fix and flips and has since spearheaded hundreds of transactions, including land subdivisions, multifamily investing, and representing both buyers and sellers selling in residential real estate transactions.

With a superpower for connecting people, Leka co-hosts a monthly meetup in the Greater Seattle Area and hosts several virtual webinars. Bringing other women together in the male-dominated real estate world brings her much joy.

Leka shares her real estate investing journey and how she was able to break through barriers to play on the same field as other investors.

Getting Started

Leka financed her first flip deal using a Home Equity Line of Credit (HELOC) on her primary residence. After gaining experience, she used the funds to do another flip, then another, then another.

Although she didn't make any money on her first flip, she made a lot of money on her second, third, and fourth flips, giving her the confidence to go out and raise money and scale her business. She knew that building a business relationship with others would require her to show a proven track record of success.

She first started raising money from friends, friends of friends, and other investors she had met since starting her house flipping career. She also raised money from individuals in her network who were looking to earn passive income.

Leka created presentations outlining her flip projects, including before and after pictures, project timelines, and results. For one project, she borrowed $100,000 from a private lender. In eight months, the lender got their initial investment back plus $30,000— she achieved a 30-year profit in only eight months.

When you start raising money, start small and do it with people you know very well. Then, begin to generate money from people you do not know that well. The capital Leka raised allowed her to participate in more than one deal at a time.

BIGGEST LESSONS IN REAL ESTATE – UNDERSTAND ALL EXIT STRATEGIES AVAILABLE

For most real estate investments, there are several exit strategies, including:

- Fix and Flip
- Refinance
- Sell
- Convert some units to condos
- Consider rebuild costs vs. repair costs

Single-family, fix and flip, and multifamily investing are often categorized in one bucket, but every project is different, and you will learn something different from each one. Once Leka started reviewing all exit strategies available, she realized what every property could be, which opened many doors.

Doing this allowed Leka to earn as much doing one deal as she did by doing multiple deals. Utilizing creative techniques, she could own and manage a property instead of fixing and flipping it.

For example, in 2015, she bought a huge property on historical lot lines. She had to decide whether to split the lot and sell off different parcels or build a new house. In Seattle, a new law allows you to put a second detached house on your property to increase the city's population in the city.

As you get more experience, you will be able to come up with several strategies. Be sure to stay informed of the latest rules and regulations for the area in which you are investing.

BE READY TO PIVOT

Having several options is critical to an investor, especially when things occur that are out of your control. The pandemic in 2020 taught many people to be prepared to quickly pivot to change your exit strategy immediately to escape failure.

And if there is anything that this pandemic needs to teach us, it is to adapt to changes and adopt measures. Another thing is being able to pivot shift and immediately change your strategy as swift as possible to escape failure.

Slow down or take a step backward to see a clearer, more in-depth picture of the situation.

BIGGEST WINS

Leka's biggest win so far came from a property she purchased in 2017 for $570,000. It was a large lot with an existing home. In the neighborhood, 4,000 sq ft homes sell for $1.5-1.6 million.

She was able to subdivide the property into three recorded lots with the county and sell those each for $500K.

In addition to the $570,000 purchase price, she invested $500,000 to remodel the house over three years.

Purchase Price	$570,000
Renovations + Subdivision Costs	$450,000
Total Expenses	**$1,020,000**
Sale of House	$985,000
Sale Lots	$1,000,000
Total Sales	**$1,985,000**

Profit – $1,985,000 - $1,020,000 = $965,000*
*minus holding costs

The success of this project gave Leka the confidence to do anything.

LOCATION. LOCATION. LOCATION.

Prior to COVID, it was anticipated that many cities such as Dallas, Fort Worth, San Antonio, Houston, and Austin would be growing at a rate close to the regular inflation rate. These places were estimated to grow as much as 2% per year (on a twelve-month basis), except for Austin, which was expected to grow at 2.24% at a minimum.

Austin is special because it is education- and technology-based. Tesla moved their biggest factory in the United States from California to Austin, Texas, joining other large technology companies such as Apple and Dell. It is anticipated to continue to grow.

In Seattle, which is home to Amazon and Google, properties are appreciating as well. A 4-unit building purchased at $1.2 million quickly increased in value to $1.6 million. Completely stripping down the units and investing $200-300K for rehab will raise the value to $2 million.

Location is key. Make sure there are some nice amenities in the neighborhood and know what class it is. Also, consider the crime rate. In appreciating areas, it OK to pay more to get what you want.

CONCLUSION

At the end of the day, it doesn't matter if it is multifamily, single-family, or a mobile home park as long as it generates cash flow. Surround yourself with people like you, who have the same ideas, and you'll be successful.

Most importantly, Leka recommends all new real estate investors find a good mentor or a leader with proven results to follow. Everyone needs help. And everybody deserves it.

ABOUT LEKA DEVATHA

Leka is a real estate developer and broker based in Seattle, WA. She moved to the US from India 14 years ago. In 2014, Leka left a corporate strategy role at Nordstrom to start Rehabit Homes, Inc., a company focused on residential redevelopment. She has since spearheaded hundreds of transactions, developing over $50M in real estate.

Leka has been featured on numerous podcasts and other media, including Business Insider and BiggerPockets. She was also a chapter contributor in the newly published book "The Only Women in The Room." To give back to the community, she hosts a popular virtual networking mixer, "Real Estate At Work," featuring prominent speakers from the industry.

CONTACT LEKA

To learn more about Leka, how she got started, and how she switched from single-family to multifamily investing, connect with her on LinkedIn. LinkedIn.com/in/Leka-Devatha-5616bb185/

The **Apartment**
Queen

We are looking for more investors like you.

Please complete The Apartment Queen™
Investor Questionnaire to be added to
our list for events and deals:
https://form.jotform.com/200207883604451

Our ideal investor is typically one of these following
Ultimate passive investors:
WOMEN with 1031 Exchange over $400K
High Net Worth Individuals
Doctors
Dentists
Engineers
Individual with 10 Years' Experience at a Company
Real Estate Brokers/Agents
Female Athletes
Aggie Women
Women CEO, Founder
Socialites
Duchess/Heiress
Individuals with Pension Funds
Endowments
Women-owned Family Offices
Those with Funds Who Support the Social Initiative
to Teach Financial Literacy to Women
Angel Investors Supporting Women

Chapter 24 – Lizzy Neutz: Getting Started in Multifamily the Right Way

Investing in multifamily properties can increase your cash flow, help diversify your portfolio, and is an excellent first step into the market. However, it is not a get-rich-quick scheme or something you should jump into without doing your due diligence.

Lizzy Neutz is the owner of Advent Equity Partners, a multifamily real estate investment company specializing in creating short- and long-term opportunities. Lizzy started her real estate investment in single-family units and transitioned to multifamily real estate investments.

She also hosts a monthly Women's Entrepreneur meetup.

Lizzy shares her experiences in getting started in multifamily.

Getting Started

Lizzy started her first business while living in Utah. After filing the business papers downtown, she went directly to the bank to open a checking account and establish credit for her business.

Like many beginning investors, she worked part-time jobs while building her investment business. She also leveraged her available credit to purchase investment properties.

After leaving Utah and moving to Kentucky, she invested in single-family markets before eventually moving into multifamily investments.

She quickly connected with others in the industry to learn more before having a multifamily deal. Any new investor should read books, watch videos, attend conferences, find a mentor and get some hands-on experience. Everyone learns differently, so do what feels most comfortable to you.

Make Important Connections

Many women believe they should first learn how to raise funds, but really they should focus on understanding the ins and outs of the trade. Attending a meetup (in person or virtual) and connecting with others will allow them to get to know and trust you. *Of course, you don't have to wait until you have a deal to begin raising funds.*

When you have zero experience, you need to gain knowledge, which builds confidence. Nobody wants to do something that they worry will fail in the end. To get some hands-on experience, find a sponsor or mentor who knows the trade and is willing to let you shadow them or even contribute some sweat equity. See how this person deals with different scenarios and how they raise money.

Recognize the difference between being scared and being unsure. Knowing that you have people in your corner who you can ask questions about handling a particular scenario will help alleviate any fear and allow you to move forward.

The real estate business is all about building rapport. When you're fundraising, consider reaching out to other syndicators and principals. If they don't currently have a deal, they may have investors who need to place capital as soon as possible.

Some syndicators may have some returns and cash sitting around, so they may invest in your deals also. Syndicators as investors would be the least difficult to work with because they understand the process.

You should also have a commercial agent who is focused on multifamily real estate investment in your circle.

ADDITIONAL RESOURCES FOR GETTING STARTED

When you're first starting your business, look into any technology that can help you. For example, there is software that allows you to make projections for your business, whether it's multifamily or something else.

You may also want to consider hiring a high-performance coach. Many can review your 90-day action plan and make recommendations. There are coaches specifically for multifamily businesses and some for general businesses. Find a program where you can make connections *and* learn.

Before signing up, ask questions to ensure it meets your expectations. Will there be one-on-one or group calls? Or Both? Is the program focused on business only? Or will it help you dig out your passions and focus on you and your personal life?.

Remember, a multifamily business doesn't happen overnight. Some people may delay starting their business until they feel financially secure. Others may keep their full-time jobs and invest passively. What works for you may not work for someone else.

LIZZY'S BIGGEST WIN

Lizzy has a passion for helping other women, and one of her biggest wins has been starting a Women's Entrepreneur group. More than 55 women attended the second in-person meetup, a considerable increase from the first meetup with ten attendees. She was elated to bring all these women together to network, connect, and learn from one another.

The meetup group is not specific to multifamily, but there are other investors in the group.

Meetups and networking groups allow potential investors to be active in multifamily while showing others how much work you put into your brand. This allows you to get to know someone and their work ethic.

LIZZY'S BIGGEST LESSON

Lizzy learned the hard way not to scale your business too fast. She merged her single-family business with a partner who had his own business and spent a lot of money on marketing. Although Lizzy felt uncomfortable with the amount of spending, she didn't stop it. They lost $10,000 because they not in a position to scale as quickly as they were marketing, did not have enough resources, and were not training enough people to help on the acquisition side of the business.

When you're starting, scale slowly and at a comfortable pace. Don't stay quiet about something that makes you feel uncomfortable.

GETTING YOURSELF TO A COMFORTABLE PLACE

If you feel overwhelmed, know that it is OK to pause. This is definitely a learning experience. Communicate with your partners and decide together what is best for the business and what you can both handle. Have regular team meetings for transparency and remain fluid to avoid becoming stagnant. You will be surprised that everything will fall naturally into place.

Embrace a little bit of aggressiveness and understand that growing pains are part of the game. Be approachable and eager to listen because communication is key.

As you move forward, keep track of what is not working to create systems and processes so you can scale your business.

ABOUT LIZZY NEUTZ

Lizzy brings her youthful energy (and love for talking) to making the necessary connections needed to get the job done and closed! She has been involved in everything from single and multifamily investing to creative financing.

She's also the founder of the *Empowering Women for the Future* networking group, which hosts a monthly entrepreneur meetup, featuring hands-on activities and speakers with an emphasis on interactivity.

CONTACT LIZZY

Website
AdventEquityPartners.com

Email
lizzy@adventequitypartners.com

LinkedIn

LinkedIn.com/in/Lizzy-Neutz-3276951b0/

Instagram

Instagram.com/LizzyNeutz

CHAPTER 25 – BROOKE JACKSON: MULTIFAMILY BROKER, LENDER, AND MOTHER

Brooke Jackson is a true believer in uplifting and supporting women, not only in commercial real estate but throughout all her interactions in the world. She is a Vice President at Newmark in Multifamily Capital Markets. Brooke has been in commercial real estate since 2010, specializing in the multifamily lending space for most of her career. Since joining Newmark, she's moved from focusing on lending on multifamily properties through Fannie Mae and Freddie Mac to placing debt on all different asset classes, still maintaining an emphasis on multifamily properties.

Brooke shared some of the challenges she faces as a mother with young children in the lending and brokerage business.

BIGGEST CHALLENGES

Getting started in the lending and brokerage industry or any other commission-based industry presents many challenges. For Brooke, the challenges were exemplified because she had to start over after the birth of each of her children.

Through her first maternity leave, she was able to take time off and work on deals to keep deal flow going. During her second maternity leave, the company's policy changed dramatically, and locked her out of all the systems so she was unable to do deals.

It's challenging for women to return to work after being unable to maintain deal flow and losing contact with customers during the leave. Many people talk about how much time off a woman can take during maternity leave, but few discuss what happens when returning to work. It's crazy to work in an industry for ten years and have to rebuild your book after taking leave for two to three months.

Fortunately, Brooke's current position at Newmark offers a fantastic brand and platform to build upon. Things are going very well, and she has picked up several business contacts from prior companies. Through

Commercial Real Estate Women (CREW), Brooke has met other women who focus on supporting women in the industry, aligning with her goals.

MENTORS AND SPONSORS

It's great to have a mentor in the industry who has more experience than you and can offer a unique take on their accomplishments and be a sounding board for ideas.

Sponsors are entirely different; you need sponsors in your corner to advocate for your achievements and capabilities. Although it would be nice to have a female sponsor in your corner, it's also nice to know you can build those relationships with men in the industry.

CREW and other women's organizations allow you to seek help and influence, but you should also be prepared to step into any male-dominated organization as well. Be ready to showcase your expertise and what you can bring to the table.

In this business, we have to negotiate, sell, talk, and be at the top of our game all the time to make a difference. Studies have shown that women who support each other will then outperform their male counterparts.

"Women Don't Ask: Negotiation and the Gender Divide" by Linda Babcock and Sara Laschever explores how women can and should negotiate for parity in their workplaces, homes, and beyond. Men have no problem asking for what they want. They take emotions out of the equation and freely voice what they believe they deserve.

Women will intuitively pick up on underlying emotions from others' expressions and actions. They listen more than 95% of the room, make everyone feel validated and heard, and allow them to disclose information.

However, women will also over sorry, overshare, and will make self-deprecating comments. Before sending an email:

- Re-read it and take away phrases like I'm sorry or I just wanted to know.

- Just get to the point and ask the question.

- Remove all the fluff and say *please* or *let me know* only once.

Softening the message reduces the effectiveness of the message. Ensure that everybody involved in a project knows what's going on, so you can make decisions together but leave out the extra stuff.

Don't be afraid to reach out to others for help, especially other women in the industry. Feel comfortable asking for a pay raise because you're doing X, Y, and Z in addition to the A, B, and C they hired you to do.

Groups like CREW are bridging that gap between women being afraid to ask and women who want to help. Also, CREW is a phenomenal advocate, publishing white papers detailing industry job descriptions and salaries.

Another great book to read on negotiating skills is "Never Split the Difference: Negotiating As If Your Life Depended On It" by Chris Voss. A former FBI hostage negotiator, Voss shares his proven approach to negotiations.

Life is a series of negotiations you should be prepared for: buying a car, negotiating a salary, buying a home, renegotiating rent, deliberating with your partner. Taking emotional intelligence and intuition to the next level, "Never Split the Difference" gives you the competitive edge in any discussion.

If you go into negotiations calmly without raising your voice, you will be better able to control the situation and make all participants feel comfortable. Honesty and sincerity are great equalizers, and technology will help us achieve that.

BIGGEST LESSON

Protect yourself when it comes to business. It's great to be a team player but be cautious that you don't over trust. Before entering a business relationship with a friend or family member, ensure that everyone involved is on the same page. Dot your Is and cross your Ts and include all of the details in a written contract. Avoid basing business decisions on personal feelings.

In discussions, remember that you don't owe anyone an explanation. Provide the facts and allow others to make their own decisions. Interestingly, you will learn a lot about brevity if you are ever involved in a lawsuit, where you present the facts without expanding on them or placing blame.

BIGGEST WIN

For Brooke, working from home at 90% capacity with two little ones under three, all while maintaining the household and keeping deals in the pipeline during the COVID pandemic has been one of her biggest wins.

She was fortunate to have help to adapt and succeed in business and life during a pandemic with lockdowns and restrictions.

Brooke is using this time to teach her girls about finance. They each have a piggy bank and understand that money buys things. She hopes to build upon that and instill the importance of finance and credit as they get older, so they have a solid footing for the future.

The wonderful thing is that we can always learn, further our education and knowledge, and share what we've learned with our little ones. Learning from our mistakes won't keep them from making mistakes, but hopefully, it will help them not make the big ones.

ABOUT BROOKE JACKSON

Brooke Jackson joined Newmark Multifamily Capital Markets, Debt & Structured Finance team as a vice president in 2019. Based in the Chicago office, Ms. Jackson originates multifamily loans nationwide. She focuses on lending directly through Fannie Mae, Freddie Mac, and HUD, and placing debt through other lender relationships, including Life Cos, Banks, and CMBS platforms.

Before Newmark, she was a vice president at SunTrust Bank, where she worked on direct lending via Fannie Mae, Freddie Mac, HUD, bridge, and construction loan programs. Before that, she underwrote CMBS loans for various major lenders at Situs.

She is currently a member of CREW Chicago (Commercial Real Estate Executive Women), REIA (Real Estate Investment Association), ULI (Urban Land Institute), and a board member of REFF (Real Estate Finance Forum).

Brooke holds degrees in Finance, Political Science, and International Business from the University of Illinois at Chicago.

CONTACT BROOKE

Email
Brooke.Jackson@ngkf.com

CHAPTER 26 – PILI YARUSI: CAPITAL RAISING

Pili Yarusi is a multifamily syndicator, owner, and operator, mostly out of Tennessee and Kentucky. She has three kids, two Bulldogs, an awesome husband, and is loving life. Pili believes in family.

She is neither an SEC attorney nor a CPA.

Pili believes in providing opportunity – not raising capital. You can have the best deal ever, but if you invest with a sponsor who doesn't manage the deal correctly, it will blow up. So, she invests with people first, whether it is other investment sponsors or investor partners.

Originally from Hawaii, Pili believes *ohana means family*. Her partners, investors, team, and everybody she touches become family to her, and that's how she treats them. Providing opportunity through that family system and communication shows that she is the right person for them.

TALKING TO FRIENDS AND FAMILY ABOUT INVESTING

Tell them what you're planning to do before you do it. When you're in the throes of learning, talk to everybody about what you're doing and put together a mock deal. Once you have all the information, think about five ways you can insert the topic into conversations. It doesn't have to be overt, just tell people, *This is what I'm doing.* Schedule a meeting with anyone who wants to learn more to have an in-depth conversation.

Then, once you have a deal, you'll have momentum with your investor base, and you can dig in deep and continue talking about what you're doing. Keep adding people to your investor list.

If you don't have an investor tracking program, use Google Sheets. List everyone you can think of who could benefit from this opportunity. Include their contact information and how and where you met them. List every time you talked because you will need this information if you do a 506B and the SEC starts asking you questions.

Communicate with your list often. Not every investor will be a good fit for your project, but you should keep them on your list for future projects for yourself and others. You can offer, *"You might not be a good fit for this one that I'm creating, but I know XYZ fund that my friend Joe is doing, or I know Pili with this syndication. I could introduce you to each other."*

GETTING STARTED

Pili and her husband Jason have an entrepreneurial and business background. They owned a restaurant in New York City and worked as bartenders and are now silent partners in that business and a brewery.

In 2013, Pili and Jason were managing a bar in New York when Hurricane Sandy hit. With a family home lifting business, Pili got her real estate license, and they started to flip homes.

However, they didn't realize that doing a large-scale project like that would take nine to twelve months. So, they began flipping smaller projects, got into wholesaling, and joined a mentorship program to build credibility.

The next logical step was to buy and hold, so they purchased two duplexes in Indiana, which gave them a phenomenal ROI. Their flipping and wholesaling business had also taken off and grown from low five figures to nearly seven figures.

Then, Jason suggested they bring large multifamily to the table. Being more risk-averse, Pili was hesitant, but they started learning about large multifamily. With a solid foundation in real estate, multifamily was a small level up, but required a lot of education. So, they found a mentor, and did exactly what was recommended. Within six months, Pili and Jason went from not knowing anything about multifamily to taking down a 94-unit in Louisville, Kentucky.

During that journey, Pili learned how to talk to people about the opportunity. She feels it's her duty to help her friends and family make money, build legacy wealth, and take care of their families.

You might not raise the capital for your project or deal, but you can still help others through your network. For anyone who thinks, *I don't have a network*, put yourself out there, start talking to people. Let them know that you're a good person, a hard worker, you're willing to put in the hours to learn how to do this the right way, and you'll start building that network.

REACHING OUT

When you first approach an investor about a deal, start with an introductory email. For example:

Hey, I want to talk to you a little bit about what I'm doing in real estate. Do you want to hop on a call?

You could share a lot of information in the email, hook them with your story, and get them into your funnel, but you miss out on that personal connection.

On a call, you can share what you do and how you do it. Find out the needs of the other party and what they're doing. Do they have the funds to invest in a deal with you? If not, you don't want to ask for them.

Keep this contact in your list. When you have a deal, send an email saying, *We currently have yada yada deal. Here's our here's all the stats. Here's the deck. If you have any questions, let's set up a call.*

ABOUT PILI YARUSI

Pili is an active Real Estate Syndicator and Real Estate Investor. In 2016, she and her husband, Jason, founded Yarusi Holdings, a multifamily investment firm. They are General Partners on over 800 units with 450 units under management. The firm repositions properties through operational efficiencies, moderate to extensive renovations, and complete rebranding.

She is also a co-host of the Multifamily Live Podcast and The Jason and Pili Project on YouTube, a project to serve those looking to lead a Fit, Rich Life.

Pili and Jason are founders of the Tennessee, Kentucky, and New Jersey Multifamily Formula Live Meet Up with over 2,200 members that focuses on Real Estate Syndication and Multifamily Investing.

CONTACT PILI

Website
YarusiHoldings.com

Email
pili@yarusiholdings.com

Find her on Clubhouse

CHAPTER 27 – ERIN HUDSON: TAKING ACTION

Erin knew she wanted to be a chiropractor and was thrilled by the idea of being her own boss and having freedom. A life-long athlete, she has always been intrigued by our body's ability to heal from the inside out. But above all, she has a love for people, and being a chiropractor allowed her to help others.

Her first wellness center opened in 2009 and within 12 months, they opened a second office. In 2017, she and her family moved to Texas, giving her the opportunity to work *on* the business instead of *in* the business. She sold her last practice in March 2020, so that she could focus her efforts in the place where her passion truly lives.

Erin shares her path to real estate investing and the lessons learned along the way.

GETTING STARTED

Erin's path to real estate started simply with her business coach demanding that she stop doing the $10-hour jobs in her wellness center and stick to being the doctor that treats patients. She quickly learned to delegate like nobody's business and her new schedule allowed her to dive into the real estate space where she was genuinely intrigued.

She spent her time looking on Craigslist for properties in Indianapolis, Indiana, because that was what she could afford. Within 12 months, she had acquired 12 properties and became addicted to it. Between patients, she would search for deals. After 24, months they had acquired 26 properties of which only two had loans on them. The rest were paid for in cash or creatively acquired.

For example, on Craigslist, she negotiated the purchase of a four-pack, and turned around and sold three of the four to friends, family members, as well doctors and patients in her office. Again, the profits from the three houses paid for the fourth.

During this time, Erin's negotiation skills blossomed. Part of their business plan was to buy four houses at about $40K each, sell three, and use the proceeds to pay for the fourth. Then repeat.

On their real estate journey, they stumbled upon multifamily investing. Like many others, they believed only the wealthy owned apartments – that was so far from the truth.

FINANCIAL LITERACY

Being raised with little financial literacy, she became addicted to learning more about finances and what the wealthy were doing. They began transitioning to multifamily and letting their investors come along for the ride.

Erin involved her then 16-year-old in real estate by offering her to put her $7000 towards a house or you can put it towards the purchase of a car. She pointed out that with the car, there are other monthly expenses like insurance and gas. Acquiring real estate, however, would pay her $600 a month.

She chose to purchase the property.

BIGGEST WIN

A gentleman from California was selling 70 homes and that happened to be in Indianapolis, Indiana. Erin and her husband pre-negotiated the price on the 70-pack, and she told him "I'll do my best to sell as many as I can. I think I'll be able to offload quite a bit of them." He agreed.

Soon after, she was invited to speak on webinar about how she acquired 12 properties in six months to give hopes to others out there.

She shared the details about the first property, showed the cap rate and cash on cash after all expenses to educate listeners on how to get in the game at a low purchase price and own it outright.

Several reached out wanting to buy deals, so Erin contacted the gentleman from California to negotiate and offered to get 18 purchase contracts in the next 24 hours if he would drop the price down $3,000 off each of the 18 properties. He laughed and said, "Sure. Good luck with that."

Within 30 days, they closed on 31 homes. With the spread between the initial purchase price and the price she sold it to the end buyers, she profited $375,000.

Instead of accepting the cash, Erin asked for inventory which equated to 12 rental properties for a bases of $1 for each property. The seller was happy because he got rid of his inventory and Erin was happy because she didn't have to pay taxes on $375,000 in earnings.

WHY REAL ESTATE?

Seeing that 90% of multi-millionaires are made from real estate, Erin thought there must be something to it. Her parents lived paycheck to paycheck, and she knew she didn't want to live a life like that. Real estate is a hard asset, and everybody needs to have a place to live.

Within three and a half years, Erin has done over 230 buy-and-sell transactions without any advertising. She attributes this success to making sure she takes care of her investors which she calls friends, so they'll come back and spread the word.

TRANSITIONING TO MULTIFAMILY

There's something really sexy about not having any overhead or a very small overhead in the real estate space. At her chiropractic office, Erin had a $50,000+ monthly overhead where she was responsible for putting food on the table for other team members. In multifamily, you link arms with others that have complementary skill sets and there's a lot of synergistic movement taking place.

Having five kids, Erin felt it was her responsibility to create a legacy and something she can pass down to her children and give them an option to work alongside them. And there's nothing better than and no better way to do it than with real estate. In the multifamily space, it's a numbers game. Think about the game of Monopoly. Do you want the little house on Vermont Street or big red hotel with 50 doors and one roof on Boardwalk?

BIGGEST LESSON

Leverage. Erin had 27 rental properties, of those only 2 were leveraged. These properties since acquiring had doubled in value ranging from $50,000 to $125,000.

After getting a taste of what this multifamily has in store for her and her family, she could kick herself in the butt for still having 21 rental properties and not transitioned in a quicker fashion to move the equity over into the multifamily arena. Erin wants to avoid selling them as a portfolio as she would rather off load five or so at a time and take part in a 1031 so she can deploy across multiple multifamily assets in order to decrease her liabilities.

Always have an exit strategy. When Erin sells these properties, she plans to put the money into the multifamily deals that her incredible partners at Quattro Capital take down in 2021.

Also, keep in mind the deferred maintenance and make-ready costs with single-family homes. The first property Erin bought was $120,000 property, and it pays $1,350 month with very few issues.

When you buy $30,000 or $50,000 homes, the deferred maintenance can eat into your profits. It seems like something always needs to be replaced, for example like a roof that happens to be a high ticket item. Every time a tenant moves out, there is high likelihood carpet and/or painting has to be done, possibly wiping out everything that you've made for that year.

BIGGEST WIN

Erin's big win was purchasing an apartment (just under $4 million), where she came in as a 25% owner using other people's money (OPM). This is one of the best ways to leverage to make massive headway in this space. You may be wondering, what did that look like? First, I posted on social media, "How would you like to be the bank, make a great return, and have it backed by real estate?" My Facebook blew up to the tune of 65 comments. The terms I shared were as follows:

7% interest only

2-year minimum

3-year maximum

Your $100K will be backed by one of my free and clear properties.

Within 48 hours, all $300k I had to bring to the table was secured. The terms worked because we had a diamond in the rough that was cash flowing 12% at time of purchase. It was a game-changing win because the property was bringing in 12%, I was paying out 7%, and the remaining 5% earning from OPM was going in MY POCKET…Pretty powerful. The best part of the story is when the first quarterly payment went to the individual (aka: lender), I got a text message that said: "Erin, I just got my check in the mail. Thank you so much for this incredible opportunity." Talk about creating a win/win. I was so thrilled to get his message simply because it reminded me that we are not begging for anyone's money; we are just offering up an opportunity.

Lastly, remember it is all about perceptional positioning. When I spoke to the individuals who all had interest in the beginning, it was about creating demand. I believe it went something like this:

Thanks for responding to the post. Wow was there an incredible demand! You were one of the first people I reached out to because at the end of the day, I get to pick who I would like to do business with. I know you, like you, and trust you. So, I thought I would make it a point to reach out to you before I touch base with the others. I want to share the terms for this incredible opportunity, which will no doubt fill up quickly. So, please circle back around when you have a moment to digest the terms." I kid you not—before I could hang up their funds were committed. Crazy, right: It goes back to the saying:

> *If you can help others get what THEY want,*
> *YOU will get what YOU want.*

I shared my BIG WIN, but I absolutely need to share my BIGGEST WIN—having the honor to be linked with the most incredibly brilliant, no-nonsense, selfless, hardworking tribe. After doing five deals together, it was a natural progression to create QUATTRO CAPITAL, and we have been on fire ever since. In the past 12 months, we have closed on nine properties.

CLOSING THOUGHTS

> *Resourcefulness is the ultimate resource.*

Find what you are good at and discover your top quality. If that is building connections, forming relationships, and raising money, don't turn over every rock looking for a deal or underwrite every property. Determine where your time is best spent. Find people whose strengths outweigh your weaknesses, and link arms with them. You will make massive traction in a much quicker fashion.

After you do the first deal, you'll find that doors open. Just a helpful tip…Don't be quick to do business with just anybody. Take time to build trust and water the relationship. For example, be sure to do background checks before entering a financial contract with a partner. Lastly, go with your gut.

Above all, take action, ladies. Put one foot in front of the other and link arms with great people and go set the world on fire. At the end of the day, that's what we were put on this earth to do.

ABOUT ERIN HUDSON

Erin is a proud mom to five beautiful children and a wife to one incredibly handsome husband. She loves being with her family in the outdoors, snowboarding, wake surfing, exploring nature, traveling the world and giving back to the less fortunate. She has run 16 full marathons around the world and thrives at any challenge.

With her family, Erin has experienced building orphanages, taking water to villages, feeding the poor, and loving on the less fortunate. Showing her children not only to be good but to do good has left a lasting impression on their hearts, which is what life is all about.

Erin is on a mission to change the trajectory of her family's life by living and teaching her children financial literacy, living their lives by design, being incredibly intentional, growing generational wealth, and leaving a massive legacy.

Website
TheQuattroway.com/Dr-Erin-Hudson

We are looking for more investors like you.

***Please complete The Apartment Queen™
Investor Questionnaire to be added to
our list for events and deals:***
https://form.jotform.com/200207883604451

Our ideal investor is typically one of these following
Ultimate passive investors:
WOMEN with 1031 Exchange over $400K
High Net Worth Individuals
Doctors
Dentists
Engineers
Individual with 10 Years' Experience at a Company
Real Estate Brokers/Agents
Female Athletes
Aggie Women
Women CEO, Founder
Socialites
Duchess/Heiress
Individuals with Pension Funds
Endowments
Women-owned Family Offices
Those with Funds Who Support the Social Initiative
to Teach Financial Literacy to Women
Angel Investors Supporting Women

Chapter 28 – Cindy Mirliss: Dissecting Apartment Operating Agreements and PPMs

Before investing in real estate, you should always have a real estate attorney review the deal and any documents before signing them. Cindy Mirliss is a Partner with Kaliser & Associates, which has a team of lawyers and support staff with extensive experience in Real Estate law, including commercial and residential. They provide legal services from the start of the transaction through the closing.

Cindy shares her *Passive Investors Guide,* which outlines what investors should look for when reviewing Operating Agreements and documents.

Create Your Investor Avatar

The first thing you should do as a passive investor is create your avatar by considering the following:

- What is your ideal investment?

- What are you looking for?

- What types of investments will you invest in?

- The cash on cash return. Is it what you are seeking? What is the minimum amount you would accept as an investment return?

- Is the deal value add or cash flow? It's important to know that so you can determine if you will get what you want out of it.

- What is the Internal Rate of Return (IRR) and the expected Cap Rate?

- How much are you being asked to invest?

- How much are you comfortable investing?

- Are accredited and sophisticated investors being accepted? In which category do you fall?

- How long are they planning to hold the property?

- What tax savings, if any, can you expect by investing?

- How large is the property? How many doors are on the property?

- Is it located in a primary market or tertiary market?

- What is the population of the area?

- What is the unemployment rate in the area?

- What's driving the economy in the area of the property?

- What is the income potential there?

This information comes into play when reviewing your Private Placement Memorandum (PPM) document. A PPM is a legal document given to all prospective investors in a real estate investment to provide full disclosure based on federal securities law requirements.

You can hire an attorney or a CPA to review your PPM. At a minimum, you should look at:

- The Manager

- The General Partner

- Have they done other deals? How many?

- Have they managed properties? How many doors?

- What kind of relationships they have?

- How many sponsors are there? Is it a team or an individual? If it's a person acting solely, do you have full confidence in that person?

- How will you invest? Will the investment be held individually? Or through an LLC? If you don't have an LLC, is that something you need to consider forming?

- Will you put it into an existing trust, or are you going to use IRA funds?

Once you determine that this deal meets your expectations and the sponsor lead on the deal has accepted or confirmed they would like to accept you into the investment, you will need to wire your funds to the sponsor.

DOCUMENTS

So, what do you do when you receive your PPM and Company Agreement? Every PPM and Company Agreement will be different depending on who drafted the document. Some will touch on different things, but all should include the following key points that you should review.

How are distributions handled? This could be one of the most important things to know. In most deals, there two classes of members. Class A includes all of the investors, and Class B is where sponsors or managers are compensated.

Find out what the split between those two classes is because that determines how the distributions will be made. Is their preference to a certain class? For instance, you may see a 90/10 split between Class A and Class B. But before Class B ever gets paid, there's some preference to Class A that must be met before the split.

Are distributions decreasing the value of your capital account? Let's say you invest $100,000 into the deal. When you receive distributions, quarterly or during operations, are they counting towards your capital account? Once the deal is either refinanced or sold, will you be made whole again?

Consider you invested $100,000 and you have received $50,000 from quarterly distributions over time. Now, the sponsors are ready to sell, so will you be made whole at that point back to 100,000? Or will you be made whole when you receive the remaining $50,000 through distributions?

Addressing Capital Calls. This certainly has come into play during the recent COVID pandemic. Capital calls may be necessary if the sponsors operating the property need cash because income hasn't been as projected. Address capital calls in the Company Agreement.

Are capital calls mandatory or discretionary, meaning if the sponsor asks for capital, are you compelled to provide that extra capital? If not, are you locked out of your shares at that point?

Or are they discretionary capital calls with no penalty if you can't contribute.

Voting Rights. Are you acquiring voting rights with your investment or are you merely acquiring distribution rights? Voting rights often coincide with the ownership percentage based on the amount you invested. But that's something you definitely want to confirm.

What are the major things do they vote on, and what is required for their votes? For instance, are members required to vote to refinance or sell the property? Is it a majority, or is it what's called a *required interest* (like a supermajority)? Typically, it's a two-thirds vote, but that's not a standard requirement, so check that in your Company Agreement.

How is a change in management handled? What if operations are moving along fine, but then a glitch occurs, or the investors are not happy with management? What is the methodology to remove a manager? What vote is required to remove a manager, and what happens when the manager is removed? Will they retain their Class A or Class B?

ASSET HOLDING PERIOD

A PPM usually includes an investment summary, business plan, and pro forma to give you an idea of the asset holding period. Is this a short-term deal where they plan to sell the property within a couple of years? Or is it a long-term hold? Make sure the terms agree with your avatar and that you're not expecting a payout before the end of the holding period

Also, be sure you know what provisions are in place in the event you need to liquidate your investment and cash out early. Is it even possible? Not always, but see how it is addressed in the Company Agreement.

Understand the method in which you can cash out. Will you need to offer the shares first to the company? Are you able to offer shares outside the company at all? How is the price set? How is an appraisal done to value your shares?

And lastly, find out when distribution will start. Typically, during rehab, there is no income, and you may be required to wait for distributions until rent is being collected. So, pay attention to whether the PPM dictates that first distributions won't start until six months or longer after ownership.

PPM vs. Company Agreement

The PPM and Company Agreement mirror each other. The PPM is the disclosure document that outlines all of the risks involved and why real estate is risky. Do not sign the PPM unless understand all of the risks.

The Company Agreement is the document that moves forward Once you close on the asset, this is basically your playbook detailing how the property will be operated. For example: what can the manager do, what rights do I have, etc.

The documents are parallel to each other, the terms are generally the same.

After the documents are created, there may be circumstances which will require changes. So, there is a possibility that an amendment to the Company Agreement can happen after the asset is purchased. Each deal is different, but the required interest, the majority of members, or all of the members may need to sign off on any changes. For example, a change in distribution is significant and would likely require all members to agree.

Other Documents for Passive Investors

When you are in a deal as a passive investor, you will typically receive a PPM, Company Agreement, and an 8-10-page Investor Questionnaire about your assets. The Sponsor uses this information to determine if you're a *sophisticated investor* or an *accredited investor*, and if you're qualified to be let into their deal.

The last document you will receive is a *Subscription Agreement*, which is your contract with the lead sponsor detailing know how much you're investing. Once the sponsor countersigns it, you wire your funds, and you're part of the deal.

The basic exemptions used to acquire commercial real estate are either Part 506B or a 506C of the SEC Regulation D.

506B is an exemption to your offering so that you do not have to go through the entire process of registering your investment. The 506B exemption prohibits you from publicly advertising your deal or having to have a pre-existing relationship with any of the investors that you accept into your deal.

The burden is on the sponsor to determine if a pre-existing relationship has been established. Typically, a pre-existing relationship is defined if there have been three encounters or three touches. Not just passing "Hellos," but three discussions, whether via email, phone, in person, or on a long zoom call. You must establish all your relationships before going under contract.

You can take an unlimited number of accredited investors (someone with a net worth of over $1 million and income over $200,000 for the last year with the anticipation of it being the same for the next two years). Also, you can accept up to 35 sophisticated but unaccredited investors. A sophisticated investor understands the nature of a real estate investment but may not meet income or asset qualifications. However, they fully understand the investment process.

A sponsor will look at a person investing $50,000 to determine if that's the full amount or a portion of their net worth. Real estate is risky, and there are no guarantees investors will get a distribution or get their money back. Obviously, there's a lot of upside potential, which is why many are interested in passively investing in real estate.

A 506C exemption gives you the ability to advertise on Facebook or a billboard, wherever you want. But you can only accept accredited investors.

If a Sophisticated Investor fills out an Investor Questionnaire, the Sponsor can accept that information is accurate.

If an Accredited Investor completes an Investor Questionnaire, the burden to determine if the applicant is accredited shifts to the Sponsor.

CAPITAL ACCOUNTS

Capital accounts are accounts in which investment funds are housed. For example, if a deal requires a $5 million capital raise and each investor contributes $50,000, all those monies are pooled into one capital account. A capital account may be used for rehab on the property, the down payment, or the difference between the purchase price and the loan amount.

A capital account requires very intricate accounting so that as distributions are made, it tracks each investor's capital account, whether it is considered a capital reduction.

OPERATING AGREEMENTS

Operating Agreements are different in the sense that they are tailored to the specifics of the deal. The Texas Business Operational Code (TBOC) dictates how companies operate in the state of Texas. If something is not addressed in the company agreement, we look to the TBOC for their parameters, which are extensive. The company agreement is based on TBOC rules but can be changed to meet your specific requirements.

For instance, typically a two-thirds vote is required to do major things with the asset within the company, but that vote can be changed at the Sponsor's discretion. There may be a higher or lower majority depending on the needs and what they foresee in operating with the asset.

SOLICITATION

Once you have a deal under contract that you're contemplating, you don't want to make promises of returns or talk about numbers, such as, "I expect to double your income through distributions in a year." Do not promise any returns or discuss numbers or financials. An investor could turn around and say, "Well, I relied on when you told me that I was going to get a 50% return on my money. And that's why I made this investment." So, the basic rule of thumb is to avoid all discussions of returns and finances.

You can certainly talk about why you think the location of a property is a good location, or the upside, employment, and the growth in the area. Or if you put a certain amount of rehab into this property, it will help increase rents. Keep it general.

Avoid talking about returns before the investor has reviewed the warning in the PPM.

CONCLUSION

Before investing in a deal, always consult an attorney who has real estate investing experience.

ABOUT CINDY MIRLISS

Cindy was born and raised in Boston, Massachusetts, and moved to Dallas, Texas, with her husband. She attended Boston University for her undergraduate degree and received her Juris Doctorate from Texas A&M University School of Law in 1995. She has worked for several of the largest firms in Dallas, including Baron & Budd, Jones Day, and McKool Smith, as well as in-house counsel for Stream Energy. Her career has given her experience in several practice areas including real estate acquisitions, class action litigation, contract and employment law, mergers and acquisitions, family law, and estate planning.

In 2015, she joined Kaliser & Associates as Lead Counsel. Cindy's practice focuses on assisting clients with commercial real estate transactions, private securities fundraising, SEC syndications for multifamily projects, as well as other commercial and real estate-related projects, and wills and estate planning.

CONTACT CINDY

Website
KaliserLaw.com/Our-Team

LinkedIn
LinkedIn.com/in/Cindy-Mirliss-0b804a80

CHAPTER 29 – ANN CONE: MULTIFAMILY AGENCY LENDER

Ann Cone is a Senior Vice President with CBRE in the Debt and Structured Finance section, which is a long way of saying she does apartment financing.

Ann specializes in government-insured loans, which are non-recourse, longer-term, and low-interest rate loans. When banks aren't lending, everyone comes to her because the government will always ensure these loans.

She recently shared with me how she helps investors get the financing they need, especially during COVID.

GOVERNMENT-BACKED LOANS

The US Department of Housing and Urban Development (HUD) also runs the Federal Housing Administration (FHA). Properties like single-family homes are FHA insured. For example, first-time homebuyers can obtain an FHA loan that says the government has vetted them. If you default on the loan, the government won't come after you. Instead, you give back the home and that's it.

The loans that Ann makes are similar, but for multifamily properties. CBRE does the underwriting and makes the loan, but it's government-insured because CBRE has verified that it's a good project with a reliable borrower and they are willing to take on the risk.

Borrowers for multifamily properties pay mortgage insurance premiums (MIP) similar to single-family Private Mortgage Insurance (PMI). Since the loan is non-recourse, if a mortgage default occurs, HUD will take the property back and you will owe no additional funds which is a huge benefit.

There are exceptions to the rules. "Bad boy carve-outs" are frequently used in commercial real estate non-recourse loans. The carve-outs make it possible for the borrower to not be personally on the hook if they default on the note (making it non-recourse) but protects investors if the borrower has conducted themselves as a "bad boy."

Examples of "bad boy" conduct include filing fraudulently-prepared financial statements and tax returns or over-leveraging the property. Some lenders are now including things like not preparing financial reports, paying property taxes late, or not having adequate insurance on the property.

Another example is when an apartment building owner makes all of the loan payments but does not use any rent money collected for maintenance or repairs. HUD will inspect your apartments every two or three years, looking for health and safety hazards. The owner will be told to bring everything up to standard. If the owner does nothing and purposely tries to circumvent the whole system, HUD will force you to sell the property.

background checks, including credit and criminal checks on all participants. They also check the United States Terrorists lists, and you can't be delinquent on any federal debt to be approved. It's in-depth review to make sure the lenders are dealing with the right borrowers.

BIGGEST LESSON

Many things have changed during Ann's 30-year career, and she has learned much through adversarial and bad times. Many people assumed COVID lockdowns would cause a financial crisis, but it's also like a natural disaster so there was a lot of uncertainty.

Ann's greatest takeaway from those difficult times is there is still so much opportunity. Her recommendation is to take a step back and look at the situation. You may worry you've lost everything, and suddenly, it becomes the greatest opportunity.

Think outside the box. What do people need during lockdowns or a recession? What are others doing? Listen to stories from others who have overcome similar problems. Know what you do best and what you love doing, and search for those opportunities. Be resilient and use what you know to help others.

Many women in multifamily work in property management and asset management, which is safe. If you do your job, you get paid. When you look at people in production. Loan originators work on commission, which has more risk. Many women shy away commission-based jobs to avoid being under the gun to produce when in fact they probably produce just as much but do not get the financial incentives.

Ann has always felt she would succeed because she would not allow herself fail and will do whatever it takes to avoid failure. The worst that could happen is during negotiation you say, "Let's do this," and the other party says, "No, that won't work for me." You either work it out or move on to the next project.

PIVOTING

During the last recession, the lending industry sort of paused for a while and there was a lot of pivoting that had to happen. For example, when more reserves were required for underwriting deals, investors could wait six months to do renovations and build income.

Banks were no longer lending, but if owners had any issues, they were going after them in foreclosure and taking everything that they've worked hard for and sell it for pennies on the dollar. Many people lost so much.

So, make sure that you are not over leveraged and be ready to pivot. Real estate goes up and down. Don't put all your eggs in one basket. Spread it out and be smart about it. Think ahead and consider the worst case scenario when you make your plans.

Also, make sure you have skin in the game. Don't have a loan that is 90% loan to value with an inflated value. When you're starting out and need some serious leverage, you would do well to bring in partners and say, "We'll give you this amount and we'll acquire this property, and we're willing to put 20%-25% down."

Don't have a scenario where you acquire a property and then assume you can quickly raise the rent $100 per month without doing any repairs. Be thoughtful on what you're doing with a forward look to know what happens if this doesn't perform as expected.

FINANCIAL RELATIONSHIPS

Deep-rooted banking relationships are critical. Even if you're not getting the cheapest and the best, it will pay off in the end. It's a hard lesson for thrifty people like Ann, but relationships building have to go both ways. You won't always get the best terms, but you will have a relationship you can count on when times get difficult.

LEVERAGE

Regular leverage is about 70-75% LTV. For anything over that, you really need to look at that asset. After that, people start incurring mezzanine debt at a higher interest rate. As long as everything is going well, they can make the payments. But as soon as there is a blip on the radar, it falls apart.

HUD FINANCING

HUD is a great program, but because the loans are government-insured, they come with a lot of bureaucratic red tape. It doesn't work well in acquisitions because the process can take six months to complete. You likely won't be able to negotiate a six-month purchase and sale agreement.

If someone has already purchased with a bridge loan or wants to re-finance., it depends on how long you want to hold the property. If you plan to hold it three to five years and then sell it, you're probably better off with Freddie and Fannie loan. HUD will do a 35-year non-recourse loan.

You have to consider the interest rates, points, and appreciation to determine the best type of loan for your property.

HUD also has a prepayment penalty to consider, which steps down every year for ten years. After that, you have no prepay penalty, no yield maintenance, and no defeasance. Defeasance is a method to reduce the required prepay fees for a commercial real estate loan.

MEZZANINE DEBT

If you're getting a bank loan that goes up to 75% LTV, you will need to come up with 25% out-of-pocket. Somebody may offer you a 10 to 15% mezzanine loan to bridge some of the 25% at a higher interest rate.

Let's say your interest on the first 75% LTV is 3%. The mezzanine loan is riskier because it's subordinate to your first mortgage. In case of default, they would get paid second. Because of this risk, you will pay a higher interest rate. However, you must be careful not to become over-leveraged when using these types of loans.

NEW CONSTRUCTION LOANS

Fannie and Freddie generally won't do construction loans. So, you'll need to get a bank loan and then do a Fannie or Freddie takeout. Ann does a lot of construction loans since HUD will do construction lending at very good terms; however, they won't do any pre-development loans. You must be able to secure your site and keep it under control for a while. When you are getting a market study done you can be getting the land appraisal and architectural drawings completed. It is very, very expensive upfront with a lot of risk during construction. While the rewards are great, the risk is as great or greater.

BIGGEST WIN

Ann has been fortunate to have many different wins. Last year, she crossed the threshold of hitting a billion dollars in financing. She has also done some affordable housing and witnessed its impact on families and people with disabilities.

Ann is a member of CREW Atlanta and had the honor of being President in 2019, which brought incredible exposure and knowledge.

Being on the lending side allows her to go to different areas, meet new people, assist them with acquisition, refinancing, or maximizing their exposure.

Finally, she has been really fortunate to work with many amazing people. And oddly enough, she learned the most important lessons from people she didn't respect or trust. That taught her to listen to her inner voice and trust her judgment.

ABOUT ANN CONE

Ann Cone is a Senior Vice President in the Atlanta office of CBRE HMF, Inc., CBRE's FHA lending division. Ms. Cone is responsible for marketing and originating FHA insured construction and permanent financing for multifamily, senior living and healthcare housing. Ms. Cone has more than 30 years in commercial real estate with an emphasis in FHA insured debt products.

Ms. Cone began her career in 1983 in Atlanta with the Center for Housing Alternatives, a non-profit organization that providing consulting and technical assistance for specialized housing for persons with disabilities. In 1986, she was promoted to Administrator, responsible for the organization's production of housing.

In 1994 she co-founded the Housing Resource Center (HRC) to provide consulting and technical services for housing for the elderly housing, persons with disabilities, and veterans. That same year, HRC was awarded the Southeastern Master Technical Assistance Advisory role for the Resolution Trust Corporation to facilitate sales to non-profit organizations for affordable housing.

In 2006, she left HRC to work on the lending side of the business with Prudential Mortgage Capital Company as Director of Originations. In this capacity, she was responsible for the origination of construction and permanent financing for market-rate and affordable multifamily properties and healthcare properties, including skilled nursing and assisted living.

Ms. Cone joined CBRE in February 2015.

Website
www.CBRE.com

LinkedIn
LinkedIn.com/in/Ann-Cone-a866b69/

The Apartment
Queen

We are looking for more investors like you.

Please complete The Apartment Queen™
Investor Questionnaire to be added to
our list for events and deals:
https://form.jotform.com/200207883604451

Our ideal investor is typically one of these following
Ultimate passive investors:
WOMEN with 1031 Exchange over $400K
High Net Worth Individuals
Doctors
Dentists
Engineers
Individual with 10 Years' Experience at a Company
Real Estate Brokers/Agents
Female Athletes
Aggie Women
Women CEO, Founder
Socialites
Duchess/Heiress
Individuals with Pension Funds
Endowments
Women-owned Family Offices
Those with Funds Who Support the Social Initiative
to Teach Financial Literacy to Women
Angel Investors Supporting Women

CHAPTER 30 – ANNA KELLEY: SMALL MULTIFAMILY AND SHORT-TERM RENTALS

Small multifamily properties, such as a duplex, triplex, or fourplex, can be an excellent real estate investment. Typically, they are easier to manage than large apartment complexes and provide higher rental income than a single-family home.

Anna Kelley, founding partner of Greater Purpose Capital, Apex Multifamily, and ReiMom.com began investing in real estate 20 years ago. She shares how she grew her rental property portfolio by investing in small multifamily and short-term rental properties.

GETTING STARTED

Anna started investing in real estate about 25 years ago. She worked at a private bank with very wealthy clients talking about retail, traditional investments, stocks, bonds, mutual funds, annuities, insurance, etc. Many of her clients made a lot of money in real estate, which piqued her interest. Over the next couple of years, she purchased a condo instead of renting an apartment. Then, she bought a house in an up-and-coming area, hoping it would turn into something.

In 2003, she had her first child. While home on maternity leave, she watched a lot of flipping house shows on HGTV. Seeing how much these house flippers were making off each deal, she thought flipping one or two houses would replace her income and allow her to stay home with her daughter.

Anna quickly discovered that house flipping is not as easy as HGTV makes it seem. The numbers they share about the deals don't cover holding costs, closing costs, transfer taxes, or realtor commissions that can eat into your profits.

The property sat on the market way too long, she spent too much money, made improvements that weren't needed, and hired unlicensed contractors, causing her to lose money on the deal.

Soon after, she had another baby, and she and her family moved from Houston, TX to Pennsylvania so her husband could open a chiropractic business.

SMALL FAMILY INVESTING

The start-up debt for opening the business, including equipment, a start-up capital loan, and buying a building left them close to $750,000 in debt. The building they purchased had commercial space on the bottom floor and two apartments on the second floor. That was Anna's first experience being a landlord with cash-flowing rental income—and it was really only done to help cover the payment on the space.

A year later, they bought a four-unit apartment building and moved into one unit with their two small children. Although the apartment was considerably smaller than the house they sold in Texas, they decided it was the safest thing to do at the time.

Anna quickly saw the power of having a little extra cash flow from the commercial space, three apartments, and the other tenants in the four-unit building. The rental income they received covered the mortgage payment for the building.

Anna soon started a new job with a large life insurance company, becoming the primary breadwinner while her husband's business got started.

In 2008, when the economy crashed, Anna purchased another four-unit building using a loan from her 401(k) account, generating another $1400-$1600 per month in income.

After 2009, she didn't buy any additional properties until around 2015, when she wanted to get serious about investing. She and her husband bought several four-unit apartment buildings and had 40-50 units.

VACATION HOMES

A trip to the beach to get away from managing the buildings, working full-time, and raising kids gave them a much-needed break but also opened their eyes to the potential income from investing in a vacation rental property. They bought their first vacation rental in Ocean City,

Maryland, as a second home they could use a few times a year. The rental income from the summer covered all of the expenses.

The success with the first Airbnb property prompted them to purchase another beach house. Additionally, some of the units in their Hershey, PA area apartments are now Airbnb rentals, and they do really, really well also.

They purchased each beach house at well below market value because they needed some work. Because these were vacation rentals, they also had to be furnished. They purchased the second beach house with the intent to fix it up, furnish, and rent it for two years to establish proven rental income. It's now on the market and should generate a $200,000 profit.

SHORT-TERM RENTALS VS. SINGLE-FAMILY RENTALS

Unlike single-family properties, which typically have tenant turnover in 6-, 12-, or 24-month periods, vacation homes can have different renters each week. Sometimes, two or more in a week, making managing the properties a full-time job, which is difficult for rental properties located in another city or state.

Anna hired a really good management company specializing in short-term rentals, handling all the bookings, cleaning, coordination, repairs, maintenance, and anything else that comes up for a flat fee. Typically, a short-term management company charges 14-15% of the rental income, but Anna negotiated a 12% fee. The process is entirely hands-off and turnkey unless there's a big expense.

LONG-TERM SUCCESS

Anna believes grit, resilience, and determination are the most important factors in long-term success for any business. But in multifamily and short-term investing, investors must have the ability to recover quickly from the unexpected bad things that happen—because they frequently do.

Tenants can be difficult; anything can go wrong in a building—major and minor repairs, flooding, fires, roof damage, etc. Contractors may be no-shows or not do a good job. You just have to have the attitude that you will make this work. Jump through every hurdle and find a way to get through it. Putting in a lot of work today will yield significant results tomorrow. Keep pushing through and seek growth every single day. Welcome challenges because those are an opportunity for growth that will make you stronger and better. Success may not be easy, but you can achieve it with hard work.

Anna was recently able to retire from AIG after working there for 20 years by replacing her income with small multifamily rentals. Now, she is ready to scale into much larger multifamily buildings because she can give it her full-time attention.

Her first large multifamily deal was a JV with two partners on a $6.5 million 73-unit right outside of Hershey, PA. She took over, turned the units, repositioned the property, and handled the asset management, allowing her springboard to continue to grow and do two other large multifamily deals. After years of hard work, she can now reap the rewards and scale up to help more people grow with her.

SETTING GOALS

While investors need to work towards goals and plan for where they want to be in 5, 10, or 20 years, they must be flexible because priorities change. Where you think you want to be in five years could change tomorrow. Focus on growth and allow yourself to pivot without any guilt. Be open to opportunity and see where it leads. Your level of success is doing what you want to do when you want to do it and enjoying it in the process. Don't be consumed with trying to figure it all out because that may never happen.

ABOUT ANNA KELLEY

Anna Kelley is the founding partner of Greater Purpose Capital, Apex Multifamily, and ReiMom.com. She is a former top-ranked Financial Relationship Manager for a Private Bank and began investing in real estate 20 years ago.

Anna has purchased, renovated, and rented millions of dollars in real estate across numerous asset classes while working full time and raising four active children. She recently retired from her corporate career after creating financial freedom through rental property investing. She has active ownership in and manages a rental portfolio valued at over $160 million and has invested in over 200 doors as a limited partner. Anna actively seeks out the best multifamily investment opportunities for her partners and investors. She coaches new investors and enjoys helping others overcome fears, increase knowledge, and minimize risks in real estate. She is an Amazon #1 Best Selling Author and runs a meetup group for Women in Real Estate.

The Apartment Queen

We are looking for more investors like you.

Please complete The Apartment Queen™ Investor Questionnaire to be added to our list for events and deals:
https://form.jotform.com/200207883604451

Our ideal investor is typically one of these following
Ultimate passive investors:
WOMEN with 1031 Exchange over $400K
High Net Worth Individuals
Doctors
Dentists
Engineers
Individual with 10 Years' Experience at a Company
Real Estate Brokers/Agents
Female Athletes
Aggie Women
Women CEO, Founder
Socialites
Duchess/Heiress
Individuals with Pension Funds
Endowments
Women-owned Family Offices
Those with Funds Who Support the Social Initiative
to Teach Financial Literacy to Women
Angel Investors Supporting Women

Chapter 31 – Amy Tiemann: Due Diligence

Amy Tiemann is the Founder and CEO of TM1 Properties, TM1 Asset Management and, Facilimax. She has been a real estate investor since 2008 with close to 1000 doors and has been full-cycle on several investments.

As a former general contractor, Amy built a national retail and multi-family construction company doing work in 16 states. She looks for value-play or hybrid deals to reposition properties to build value or combine technology with her property management company to bring value to a deal.

Getting Started

Before investing in apartments, Amy was a general contractor for 12 years. In 2010, she started investing in multifamily properties and was the general contractor for the rehab projects.

Soon, other investors asked Amy's company to renovate their apartment complexes. Since then, they have renovated close to 60 apartment complexes in Austin, San Antonio, and Bryan/College Station.

She was often asked to walk a property and help potential buyers perform their due diligence because of her experience. Amy shares the most important things she looks for when conducting due diligence on a large commercial property.

Property Age

When purchasing a property, investors will know the property's age, but many don't understand that this can tell you a lot about the property based on the codes that were in effect when it was built.

For example, if you buy anything built in the 1960s, the sewer lines will likely be cast iron, which will eventually fall apart. Confirm with the previous owner if they replaced the sewer lines since the original construction.

If the lines haven't been replaced, there are often repairs to portions of the lines. So, there will be cast iron, then PVC, then a bucket, or something else that may fall apart.

PLUMBING

For a multifamily property, find out if there are cut-offs for every building. If not, you will have to turn the water off for the entire property to fix a leaking toilet in one unit.

When inspecting the plumbing, snake the lines and get a video to see what is happening in low areas. Look for roots that could backup your property. If you see roots in there, it's already backing up.

Also, look for any major sewer lines breaks and any Ts. If the camera line does not go to the street because there's a T, that is an issue you need to plan to fix because it was cause stuff to catch and back up the lines. It's a relatively easy fix for your plumber to turn the Ts into Ys.

There will not be a plumbing design map for your property showing where the water and sewer lines are running. Property maintenance might know some of this if they've had to fix the lines previously.

It's a good idea to budget plenty of "oops money" for things like this. Allow at least a 10% contingency for plumbing issues, and 20% if the property is older.

ROOFS

Always look at the condition of the roof and know what materials were used. Consider the age of the property when building your contingency plan.

A general contractor can probably tell by looking what kind of roof it is. Thermoplastic Polyolefin (TPO) roofs typically leak, even if installed by a great roofer.

Also, be aware that most companies won't honor other company's warranties.

Electrical

Most buyers don't always know to check whether the electrical system has aluminum wiring. From about 1968 to 1973, there was a copper shortage. Also, about 10 years ago, the price of copper went up so high that people were stealing it out of A/C lines.

As a result, properties were built using aluminum wiring, which is not the best conduit out there and poses a fire hazard. An inspector should catch it, but you should be aware that there may be a need to retrofit every apartment with aluminum wiring. Each outlet in the kitchen, bathroom, etc. is different.

Always inspect the breaker panels. If they look bad to you, they will to the inspector as well. Include costs for replacing breaker panels in the Cap Ex budget. Also consider expenses for pulling permits, etc.

Finally, some properties have big, long meter boxes. In the 1980s, all of the meters for a property were put together in one box without considering that meter sizes may change in ten years. In this situation, if one meter fails, all ten meters must be updated to bring it up to code. That's close to $20,000 you will spend because there's a life safety issue for a tenant paying $800 a month.

Mechanical

Does the property have a chiller? Some used to have chillers that were replaced with P-Tech units (small wall units). They don't cool well, so basically, everybody stays in living room because the bedrooms are too hot.

Chillers may be a little expensive, but wall units will leak everywhere and ruin your exteriors and cause cracks in the concrete sidewalks, which some lenders will require you to repair.

When you have a property with a pre-chiller system, there is duct work in every unit. There are no air handlers, but there is space for them. If you want to retrofit these, you need to make sure the duct work is in good condition and patch any holes.

Changing this setup to split systems is a lot easier than going from nothing to split system because you already have the space built out.

HVAC

It is essential you have an HVAC contractor inspect the HVAC system. This is one of the biggest capital expenses, especially in Texas, where you will be replacing units frequently. An HVAC contractor can tell a lot about the unit based on how it sounds or looks, such as what's going on in the unit, what the rattling noise is, or the unit's age.

Consider more than the age of the AC unit. 80% of HVAC problems are electrical, not the unit itself. Your AC technician should check that the connectors, feeds, and drops all lineup. If the AC does not have a disconnect, you will be required to install one.

Also, some cities, like Austin, Texas, do not grandfather properties and want them updated. If you need to repair or replace an AC, you will have to pull a permit and install a disconnect (about $400) to bring it up to code.

During your due diligence period, if you feel confident that you are going to buy this property, this is a great time to do an asset management inventory. While you're looking at all of the units, write down the serial numbers.

The serial number will tell you how old the unit is so you can plan to replace anything over 15 years, for example. It will also tell you what type of Freon the unit uses. If it is an R-22 unit, you can't only replace the condenser; you will have to replace the air handler on the inside, which can be $1100 or $1200, depending on the labor costs.

In summary, be efficient with your due diligence period and capture valuable asset information when walking the property or each unit. Look at all of the appliances, toilets, and A/C units. Recording the serial numbers will allow you to determine if it's under warranty or not, which helps you budget for those costs and prioritize replacing any items.

CODE ENFORCEMENT

Code requires you have to have an on/off switch for your dishwasher. If maintenance needs to repair or replace the dishwasher, they must be able to turn it off and unplug the wires.

Remember, tenants are more than happy to call code enforcement about your property. They'll go through their entire unit and report anything not up to code.

GUTTERS

Besides the roof and foundation, you should also be looking at the property's gutters. They should be away from the building so that the water doesn't run down, causing problems for your foundations.

Clean out leaves from the gutters to avoid backup problems and inspect all the flashing under the gutters. When leaves collect in the gutter, the water backs up and starts ruining the roof.

BALCONIES

Balconies on buildings that were built before 1985 will not meet code. The simplest and least expensive solution is installing corner posts and supporting it from underneath, so the load is carried by the ground.

A general contractor can walk the property and spot balconies that look bad. Look closely at staircases that go up to the second floor. Typically, people don't flash where the staircase meets the balcony very well. Water runs through there and erodes it away. If you leave it long enough, your staircase will eventually fall over and become detached from the building.

DRAINAGE

During your 30 to 60-day due diligence period, visit the property when it's raining. Observe if there is ponding water that is not draining. Clear any blockages and replace any systems that are not draining properly to avoid water entering any units.

DRIVE THE PROPERTY AT NIGHT

Most buyers will view a property during business hours when it is light outside. You should always drive by the property at night to see how much traffic goes by, if there are drug dealers or prostitutes, and if the property is well lit.

If you can, plan to add lights and find the best locations to place security cameras, especially if infrared is required.

Including security in your cap-ex budget is very important. Ensure you drive by or walk the property at night to ensure you include everything you need in your budget.

DUE DILIGENCE PERIOD

Typically, buyers have 30-45 days to conduct their due diligence. Plus, you have more time after that for extensions. Schedule time for each contractor to view the property during the due diligence period. Remember, some contractors may need to come out multiple times, so schedule these walkthroughs as soon as possible.

If the property is occupied, it may be good to schedule as many as you can on the same day to avoid being too intrusive.

During this review, you will want to use a separate checklist for vacant and occupied properties. Budget make-ready costs for vacant properties and check for life safety and major repairs needed on occupied properties.

Also, if the deal is delayed, like what happened to many during COVID in 2020, keep checking on the property until you close. A lot can happen in four to eight weeks.

Due diligence requires patience, hard work, and professionals who can advise their clients. When done correctly, you will have a thorough understanding of the building's construction and maintenance history.

ABOUT AMY TIEMANN

Amy has a long history in construction – her grandfather started a glass company in 1960. After her father took it over in 1972, Amy spent a lot of time going to job sites with him. Amy graduated from Purdue with a degree in Organizational Leadership and returned home. Her father asked her to join the family business, but she had other plans.

Amy made the move to tech and worked in HR for major companies such as Phillips, IBM, and Applied Materials. Suddenly, in 2001, she found herself going through a painful tech downturn, with the burst of the dot-com bubble. After surviving several rounds of layoffs, Amy found herself burned out in tech and HR. At the time, her husband was running a small construction company, giving her the opportunity for a new challenge in a field in which she was knowledgeable.

Over 12 years, she built Tiemann Construction into a national, retail construction firm servicing 16 states. From there, the company pivoted to multifamily renovations – along with a real estate investing arm of the business in 2008. Tiemann Construction was named the multifamily vendor of the year for the Austin and San Antonio market for a large real estate investment association in 2013.

Amy's first multifamily investment was in 2010. Amy and her husband became active in multifamily investing and real estate investing while managing their construction business. By 2015, she decided to focus full-time on real estate investing and went out on her own in 2017.

CONTACT AMY

Websites
InvestingWithAmy.com
TM1Properties.com

Facebook
Facebook.com/TM1Properties

LinkedIn
LinkedIn.com/in/Amy-Tiemann-911b566

Chapter 32 – Kristy Siple, CPA: Tax Information for Syndicated Properties

As an investor, you should understand the importance of monitoring your finances and managing your tax obligations. Also, know how to structure your business so that it will qualify for the maximum tax deductions. When you buy, flip, or rent property to others, the bookkeeping and taxes become more complicated.

Financial statements, 1031 exchanges, and tax deferral transactions can be overwhelming to an investor. Having a good CPA with real estate knowledge will ensure that your business is not adversely affected by tax code changes and that you are taking advantage of all available tax credits and deductions. When tax liabilities decrease, profits increase.

Kristy Siple, CPA, shares some frequently asked questions she receives from investors and provides some examples of the tax benefits available.

Real Estate Assets and Leasing (REAL) Reform Act of 2018

In 2018, there were many changes to real estate tax laws, most notably:

- Cost study report to segregate asset cost value leads to accelerated depreciation

- Capital improvements can be eligible for accelerated depreciation

- Sale of real estate can be deferred by 1031 exchange - does not apply to partnership interest

- Sale of real estate can be deferred by investing in opportunity zone property

- Cash received (rents, etc.) during the holding period is typically tax-free

COST SEGREGATION STUDIES

Cost Segregation is a tax deferral strategy (approved by the IRS) that analyzes a commercial property and reclassifies certain assets as tangible personal property. Examples of these assets may include wall coverings, electrical wiring, plumbing fixtures, and floor coverings. Personal property depreciates over 5, 7, or 15 years unlike real property, which typically depreciates over 39 years. Classifying more assets as personal property allows building owners to reap the benefits of shorter depreciation periods and capture accelerated (bonus) depreciation deductions.

Individuals who have tax and engineering expertise usually conduct cost segregation studies. They will go to the property to see if you have specific amenities in the complex and interior units. Then, they break down costs into categories that determine how much the property owner will be able to write off in the first year and how much of that cost will depreciate.

The findings of a cost study report will indicate that about 30% of the acquisition price is "eligible property for cost bonus depreciation." So, a multifamily property purchased for $10 million will have about $3 million in eligible bonus depreciation costs.

ACCELERATED DEPRECIATION

Bonus Depreciation (also known as accelerated depreciation) accelerates that cost, allowing the property owner to deduct that amount in the very first year of the purchase or the very first year they are renting the property. This will result in a significant loss on a K-1 — more than any other year you will hold this property interest.

Many investors find the bonus depreciation advantageous because it allows them to save money while holding the investment. Remember, this is a tax loss, *not* a cash flow loss.

After a building is purchased, there is a plan for capital expenditures that will occur probably Year 1 or 2 and may also be available for accelerated depreciation. Although you many not include these expenses in the cost study from the 1st year report, capital improvements may be available for consideration of bonus deprecations.

So what is the role of CPA in this process? Typically, the CPA will review the cost and help the asset manager or owner determine what is eligible for a tax deduction.

Other things such as repairs and maintenance will be regarded as operational expenses and not subject to recapture.

1031 Exchange

1031 exchange (from Section 1031 of the U.S. Internal Revenue Code) allows investors to avoid paying capital gains taxes when selling an investment property by reinvesting the proceeds from the sale in a property of like kind with an equal or greater value within a certain period.

A **Like-kind property** is defined based on its characteristics, not its quality or grade, creating a broad range of exchangeable real properties. For example, you can exchange vacant land for a commercial building or industrial property for residential property. Buyers must hold the property for investment, not for resale or personal use, typically for a minimum of two years.

Tax deferral is the main benefit of doing a 1031 exchange instead of selling one property and buying another. Defer capital gains tax frees up more capital to invest in a replacement property.

Opportunity Zones

To encourage capital investment in economically distressed areas, corporations can attract investors into multifamily real estate through opportunity funds.

Investors must invest through an Opportunity Fund to qualify for this program's tax incentives and funds must be used to either invest in new construction or substantial rehabilitation to properties. For building improvements, an Opportunity Fund must invest more in a building's restoration than was originally invested in purchasing the building. In either case, you must complete all construction or rehabilitation work within 30 months after a property is purchased.

So, if you are trading in the market and want to defer any capital gains from stock, consider investing your proceeds from that sale in opportunity zones. These have been around for a short time and are something that people are looking to when starting to invest. Be aware that there may be a waiting period to receive cash in the development of an opportunity zone. You want to hold them for at least ten years because the gains can become taxable if you sell before then.

So, there are several areas of opportunity for tax deferrals beyond real estate but can vary depending on the market in which you are investing. It is important that you perform your due diligence and speak with a tax specialist.

CASH RECEIVED

Finally, the most important thing to discuss is that while you're holding the multifamily property, you're going to see cash returns. The asset managers will determine if those are monthly or quarterly. The cash you are receiving cash or holding is not taxable during the holding period. So property owners wonder, "What does that mean to me and what does the money really represent?" As the property produces income and plenty of cash flow, the asset managers will consider a payout to the investors.

TAX CONSEQUENCES FOR ACTIVE VS. PASSIVE INVESTORS

Below is a summary of the differences between active and passive investors:

PASSIVE INVESTORS

- Passive investor does not materially participate in day-to-day activities

- Risk in investment is limited to the amount of capital contributed

Active Investors

Risk beyond contributed capital (i.e., personal guarantees, perform-ance risk, legal and regulatory responsibilities)

As a passive investor, you will not have a say in the property, will not be tasked to determine who the tenants are, and will not decide how to operate the property.

But if you are actively involved and immersed in these activities, this is commonly referred to as mature (active) participation, meaning that you:

- Will sign the mortgage statement

- Regularly take part in property management

- Participate in operations in terms of decision-making.

- Dealing with issues that might arise.

- Performing the due diligence to consider what the property should be.

- Have performance risk according to your signed agreement.

- Responsible for regulatory requirements.

- Have skin in the game and have more to lose.

It doesn't matter if you are an active or passive investor because your K-1 will be represented on your tax return, depending on how you class-ify yourself.

For example, say you invested in a property that a $100,000 investment. As a passive investor, we'll assume that you have a full-time job, are invested in a stock market, and have another source of income. You are also looking for that opportunity to use that bonus depreciation as best you can.

So in this scenario, on your first K-1, about $65,000 will be available to you because of the cost study.

But the material (active) investor will see that income or loss offset their income.

Income and Taxation – Holding Period				
Passive Investor			**Active Investor**	
Earned Income	200,000		Earned Income	200,000
Interest, dividends, stocks	15,000		Interest, dividends, stocks	15,000
Passive loss, i.e., Real Estate K-1	(65,000)		Active loss, i.e., Real Estate K-1	(65,000)
Passive Loss Limitation – Carry-Forward	65,000		Passive Loss Limitation – Carry-Forward	N/A
QTR Checks from Real Estate K-1 Holding Period	12,000 tax-free		QTR Checks from Real Estate K-1 Holding Period	12,000 tax-free
Estimate Annual Tax	64,600		Estimate Annual Tax	40,440
1st Year Invest	100,000		1st Year Invest	100,000

Income and Taxation – Year of Sale					
Passive Investor			Active Investor		
Earned Income	200,000		Earned Income		200,000
Interest, dividends, stocks	15,000		Interest, dividends, stocks		15,000
Gain on sale of real estate – 5 years	70,000		Gain on sale of real estate – 5 years		70,000
Passive Loss – Carry-Forward	(65,000)		Passive Loss– Carry-Forward		N/A
Real Estate Cash Receive	170,000 tax-free		Real Estate Cash Receive		170,000 tax-free
Estimate Annual Tax	38,600		Estimate Annual Tax		75,800
Tax Saved	26,000		Tax Saved		35,360

However, most individual, when they are looking at investing in real estate, it is complex to get their head around of what is happening and understand when they cannot see it necessarily all at the same time.

IS IT A REQUIREMENT TO HAVE AN ENGINEER DO THE COST STUDY?

There are a few options for having a cost study done. You could hire an engineering firm or use a certified appraiser. An engineering firm will likely cost more. A certified appraiser may not be as detailed as the engineer, but the cost will be about half what an engineering firm charges.

A third approach is available for properties in the $1-5 million range. A CPA who is knowledgeable about cost segregation rules can also allocate those costs in the first year.

It would be more beneficial to the property owner if there was an audit to confirm the price range.

KRISTY'S BIGGEST LESSON

Kristy's biggest lesson in real estate investing is twofold:

1. Do your due diligence and educate yourself so that you understand what you're doing and where you're going.

2. Be flexible. Even if you do your due diligence, things don't always go the way you think they should. Be able to respond to different situations and make modification so the deal still can be successful.

ABOUT KRISTY SIPLE

Kristy Siple is the Principal-Owner of KLS CPA, and she is a Certified Public Accountant and a member of the AICPA, TSCPA, and Dallas Chapter of the TSCPA. She graduated from the University of North Texas in 1995 with a BS in Accounting and has been licensed as a CPA in Texas since 2004.

Real estate has been a large part of her history and current practice. Kristy's goal is to help investors understand the tax matters around their real estate investment strategy and plan for their future goals. In addition to general personal and business tax services, KLS CPA provides tax returns and investor K-1s for syndicated properties, UBIT tax returns for IRA investors, and consultation with entity structuring.

CONTACT KRISTY

Website
KLSipleCPA.com/home.html

Email
kristy@klsiplecpa.com

Phone
(972) 895-3834

CHAPTER 33 – CHAT STEINWALD: COMMERCIAL REAL ESTATE INVESTING

Chat Steinwald focuses on multifamily and commercial real estate investing. Her mentor, whom she met in 2018, is Multifamily Guru and Investor, Rod Khleif. Since joining Rod's program, Chat has become a Limited Partner in more than 700 apartment units and a General Partner in 208 units.

She has quickly discovered the potential and opportunities for solid returns in multifamily residential investing by aligning with reputable partners and helping others to discover the same.

Chat co-founded Multifamily Women's Mastermind, a women's group focusing on multifamily investing with over 250 very successful and active members who share knowledge, collaborate, and network while focusing on the multifamily investing space.

After her husband passed away, she faced many challenges. She sold her house in Brentwood, CA, where she lived with her family for over 20 years, closed her spa business, and now focuses solely on her thriving multifamily real estate investing business, allowing her to travel all over the United States.

Chat is passionate about life, loves to spend time with her son, friends, and family. She is on the Advisory Board for OUR GRIEF Support Center that helps those who have had a profound loss in life get support and find hope again.

GETTING STARTED

Chat Steinwald came to America with the vision that she would be a successful person. She attended Vanderbilt University as an exchange student. Following graduation, she got a job at Dun & Bradstreet in Los Angeles, California.

After marrying and having a baby, Chat wanted to be a proactive parent, so she gave up her corporate job. She opened a spa so that she could run the business. Her husband, who had a CPA firm in Brentwood, helped her analyze and set it up, and it was very successful.

Suddenly, Chat's husband passed away. He had always been was the one who handled their financial and legal business. He always took care of Chat, even after he was gone.

Unable to sleep, Chat would watch TV late at night. She signed up for a $20,000 *How to Make Money in Real Estate* course to accelerate her studies. However, it turned out to be a scam, and she lost her money. Because of that lesson, she is vigilant about researching before signing up for any classes or coaching.

She would also listen to podcasts and found "The Lifetime Cash Flow Through Real Estate Podcast" by Rod Khleif. She purchased a VIP ticket to attend his live event, which changed her life.

It didn't come easy because she was still broken, very cynical, skeptical, and reluctant to talk to just anybody.

BIGGEST LESSON

Chat attends several events, boot camps, meetups, and co-founded a women's mastermind group that now has over 250 members and has learned a lot from each of these.

It is critical you know who you're dealing with. Chat is an accredited passive investor and does not currently have plans to syndicate. it is very important that the Sponsors, the group of people that are running a deal, are knowledgeable and vetted.

Also, the numbers must be right for her to invest.

Because the people she met at the boot camps, events, and on podcasts were so generous in offering their help in the industry, she quickly learned how to discern a good deal from a not-so-good deal.

Looking back, Chat was apprehensive about coming into this business. She had many opportunities to buy apartments, and she had the cash to pay for them. But she suffered from paralysis by analysis. She passed on deals that are currently cash flowing.

If you feel confident and you know the ins and outs of the deal, go for it.

Sponsor and Passive Investors

Whether you are sponsoring a deal or are passively investing, you should be able to look at the underwriting and understand the following:

- What assumptions are they using?

- What's too aggressive?

- What's reasonable for that market?

- What's the exit cap rate?

With a degree in accounting and experience at Dun & Bradstreet, Chat knows about numbers and how to analyze deals. Still, she relies on a mentor to help her better understand the ins and outs of the deal.

There may be a high cost for a mentor, but you will definitely see a return on your investment. Chat has mentors for her personnel mindset and her businesses.

If you find somebody that is already at the level you want to be at, then bring some value to their life, whether it's helping them underwrite deals or bringing in money. Everybody wins.

Biggest Win

Chat's greatest personal success and biggest is raising her son as a good human being.

In business and real, she has become friends with so many great people in the industry who are incredibly generous with their time and knowledge. The majority of the people in the multifamily investing space have an abundance mentality and are willing to give their time and help each other.

ABOUT CHAT STEINWALD

Chat Sarmiento-Steinwald is a native of the Philippines. Her dream as a child, like many other Filipinos, was to live in America. To pursue her dream, she worked as an Accounts Analyst with Philippine Airlines for two years to use her travel benefit to migrate to the USA. Armed with one hundred dollars, a degree in accounting, and a fearless drive for the American dream, she arrived in Los Angeles at the age of 23. After landing a job at Dunn & Bradstreet as a Trust Accountant, becoming a mother, and opening an award-winning spa, she decided to focus on multifamily and commercial real estate investing.

Chat began investing in real estate as a necessity after the sudden death of her husband. She has become a limited partner in 800 apartment units and a GP in over 400 units.

Chat also co-founded a women's group focusing on multifamily investing called Multifamily Women's Mastermind with over 500 very successful and active members in the industry. She is also a chapter leader and host for a meetup in the Los Angeles area. Chat loves to travel and loves to give back and plans to do more philanthropic works in the near future.

LinkedIn

LinkedIn.com/in/Chat-Sarmiento-Steinwald-a8aba2191/

Instagram

Instagram.com/Chat.Sarmiento.Steinwald/?hl=en

The **Apartment** *Queen*

We are looking for more investors like you.

**Please complete The Apartment Queen™
Investor Questionnaire to be added to
our list for events and deals:**
https://form.jotform.com/200207883604451

Our ideal investor is typically one of these following
Ultimate passive investors:
WOMEN with 1031 Exchange over $400K
High Net Worth Individuals
Doctors
Dentists
Engineers
Individual with 10 Years' Experience at a Company
Real Estate Brokers/Agents
Female Athletes
Aggie Women
Women CEO, Founder
Socialites
Duchess/Heiress
Individuals with Pension Funds
Endowments
Women-owned Family Offices
Those with Funds Who Support the Social Initiative
to Teach Financial Literacy to Women
Angel Investors Supporting Women

CHAPTER 34 – SANDHYA SESHADRI: NEGOTIATING SECRETS REVEALED

Sandhya Seshadri has a bachelor's and master's in Electrical Engineering as well as an MBA. She worked on large programs at Texas Instruments for over a decade, and she learned about contract negotiations with vendors along the way.

Growing up in India, she was raised to bargain for everything. For example, when shopping, immediately offer half of the asking price for an item and never, never pay full price.

Even if she ends up paying the same price, if the seller tells her it's 50% off, that's more appealing to Sandhya.

Sandhya shares some negotiating tips for multifamily investing.

NEGOTIATING IS IMPORTANT

Many buyers won't negotiate because they're afraid the seller will say, "No." Or worse, "How dare you ask for that?" Others may say very nicely, "Absolutely not."

If the price is non-negotiable, find out what terms are negotiable. You can always find a way to meet in the middle.

When buying single-family homes, Sandhya always uses real estate agents because they have a good pulse on what the seller's lowball price is and what would be an insult. Then, she can add something to the lowball price and make an offer.

For example, she would say *pending a new roof* or *pending a fully working sprinkler system*. She always starts at the lowest price she can.

On a recent multifamily transaction, she was in best and final. After negotiating a low price and requesting a new roof, she calculated the increased cost of insurance, the cost to replace the roof, and the next buyer's perception if she didn't replace it.

Be sure to establish a threshold and don't try to move it to please others. Ultimately, it'll put you in financial disaster, whether it's your personal funds for a single-family property or you have passive investors for a multifamily property. Know your ceiling and come well below that for your initial offer to ensure you have wiggle room as you go through multiple rounds of negotiations.

MAKING UP THE DIFFERENCE

If the seller rejects your offer, find out if they are open to a counter-offer. If so, calculate the difference between your threshold and their asking price. Let's say you are $100,000 off from the asking price, which the seller does not want to lower. Consider what terms you could ask for instead. Here are some ways you can squeeze the $100,000:

1. **Request extra time to do an early assessment**. Bring your contractors with you to accurately price repairs. If you find something that may cost $50,000 to repair, request that those repairs be made prior to closing the deal.

2. **Request an extension**. Instead of closing in 45 or 60 days, price out extensions to either get them free or at a very low cost. This allows you more time to find things at the property you can use to negotiate more contracts, etc.

3. See if the broker or lender will reduce their commission.

4. Get additional quotes for insurance.

5. Protest the taxes.

6. Request termite and pest control treatments are done the day before taking control of the property.

Every little thing adds up to get you to that 100 K to close the gap. So, always search for things to negotiate that will reduce your costs other than price.

Techniques to keep the other party negotiating

When you see value in a property and want that asset, say things to the current property owner such as, *"You've done such a great job with this property. I really love this property. I believe I can take it to the next level by doing this, this, and this."*

Some direct questions you can ask are:

- What will it take?

- How can we make this work for both of us?

- What is your pain point?

In a recent multifamily deal that Sandhya acquired, the seller needed to hit a certain number from an accounting standpoint and could not accept a number below that. Using a creative way of structuring the deal, they made up the $200K difference through seller financing that gave the seller a pref return.

In multifamily, the seller does not usually need to sell the property urgently unless it's a forbearance deal or something like that. But even then, the buyer won't know if one of the sellers has a life event, such as a divorce, causing them to want to get out of the property quickly.

Once the seller decides to get out of the property, it's just a matter of who will be the buyer (or the scapegoat) to pay that high price for it.

This individual had 1031 exchanged several single-family rentals to purchase a large multifamily property. He was located out of state but had one property in Texas with no one boots on the ground to help him except the property management company.

There were constant problems and repairs that he could not super-vise regularly. The quality of the repairs was poor, and it was expensive, causing him to want to get out of it quickly because it was becoming a headache to asset manage remotely.

So, he became part of the financing with a low preference rate of 4% and no equity split, like a new Class "C" (Class A is a typical passive investor who is the first to get paid; Class B includes the GPs). As soon as we paid the Fannie loan payment, he would receive his 4% as the additional "loan", and only then would everybody else get paid.

Somehow, that made him agree to sign the deal. They found a way to reach his sale price by giving him a 4% pref return with no equity split or anything else in the deal. It was basically a low-interest supplement loan for the buyer.

There's always a way; you have to keep searching. Owner or seller financing is another approach that may work. Often, the property owner wants to free themselves from the hassle of managing the property, and seller financing offers them an option to feel like they still own it while earning a comparable return.

But you must decide in your head: *I want to make this work. I like this deal enough that I want to make this work. This is my threshold.*

GET IT IN WRITING

Put everything in writing. If you have a verbal agreement, follow up with an email confirming everything you agreed to with the other party. Make any edits so that there are no misunderstandings. Then, make the offer and get your legal team involved when the LOI is accepted.

Before speaking with a seller, create a list of questions before you start the conversation and use it as a checklist as you talk. To ensure you don't forget something, block your questions together under categories.

For example, financing equity share, what are the negotiable terms non-negotiable terms? Is there an urgency to sell by a certain date? What are the pain points? What will he/she not come down on? What are some questions to ask that your accountant would want you to include if you were having this conversation with him/her? It's also a good idea to talk with your lawyer before you start negotiating. Ask, *What am I allowed and not allowed to do?*

Consider what you can negotiate from your lender's point of view. What would give you a better term? Possibly, a greater LTV. If you want 80% LTV, for example, reduce the Interest Only period. If you raise more money and only do a 70% LTV loan, maybe you'll get more Interest Only, which gives you better cash flow initially because there's a deep value add.

Speak with your trusted experts about things you can negotiate to make your list. It's much easier to negotiate when you're mentally organized and go through your list and check off all these points.

You can also drive by a property you're interested in purchasing and look for things on your checklist. Record a video while speaking about what you are seeing, which is easier than pulling over and writing or typing your notes.

Add that video file to your folder for that project. If you decide not to go further with the property, delete the video or put it in a *Deals not pursuing* folder. Then, you'll always have it. Since the same properties come up for sale every three years, you now have a history of that property.

Try to start recording your video with something distinctive about the property and say the property's name, such as: *We're touring property X, which has this many doors in this city. The whisper price is $Y, and the property is listed by this broker.*

This allows you to determine if the property is worth a second look.

ABOUT SANDHYA SESHADRI

Sandhya Seshadri has invested as a Limited Partner, Key Principal, or General Partner in 3000+ doors totaling $200M in assets throughout the United States.

Sandhya has been a leader in the equities markets for over 20 years and had moved into commercial real estate due to the tax advantages and the ability to uniquely "force appreciate" each asset. It's become her mission to help other people capitalize on all of the benefits of real estate investing.

Sandhya is active in the Dallas-Fort Worth Multifamily real estate community and has a network of investors throughout the United States. She has shared her inspiring story, knowledge and investment criteria on multiple real estate investing events and podcasts.

Sandhya is passionate about personal and professional growth. She is active in multiple mastermind groups focused on apartment investing to continuously stay abreast of these changing times, and their impact on multifamily.

Sandhya has lived in Dallas-Fort Worth for over 30 years, and this is her primary market for investments. Her knowledge of the local market and neighborhoods makes her the ideal "boots on the ground" asset manager for properties in Dallas.

Sandhya has a bachelor's and master's degree in Electrical Engineering as well as an MBA.

Contact Sandhya

Website
Multifamily4You.com

The Apartment
Queen

We are looking for more investors like you.

Please complete The Apartment Queen™
Investor Questionnaire to be added to
our list for events and deals:
https://form.jotform.com/200207883604451

Our ideal investor is typically one of these following
Ultimate passive investors:
WOMEN with 1031 Exchange over $400K
High Net Worth Individuals
Doctors
Dentists
Engineers
Individual with 10 Years' Experience at a Company
Real Estate Brokers/Agents
Female Athletes
Aggie Women
Women CEO, Founder
Socialites
Duchess/Heiress
Individuals with Pension Funds
Endowments
Women-owned Family Offices
Those with Funds Who Support the Social Initiative
to Teach Financial Literacy to Women
Angel Investors Supporting Women

About Kaylee McMahon and The Apartment Queen

ABOUT KAYLEE MCMAHON "THE APARTMENT QUEEN"

What gets Kaylee out of bed every day is her determination to create financial independence and a space for those in codependent and toxic relationships, which hampers their ability to visualize and manifest an amazing reality.

Her company, The Apartment Queen, is changing the face of multi-family by involving more women as powerhouse operators, key principles, and limited partners. Kaylee's vision is to create 1 billion female SheVestors and "givers" by 2030.

Kaylee has done home flipping, note buying, active/passive investing in apartments, and sometimes is her own lender. She feels that to be truly confident in giving advice, one should have experience and knowledge of the subjects they are advising.

Kaylee has purchased over $68.2 million in multifamily real estate as a General partner and principle. She sold over $3 million in residential real estate before transitioning into her current full-time syndication role.

Originally from Portland, Oregon, she founded the Women Who Invest Wednesday networking group in Dallas, which is also virtual. She is also the host of the #1 Leading Ladies podcast, where she interviews kick-ass women who are disrupting their industry to share the REAL story of how they got where they are.

She is currently developing the Shevest app, which provides a simple and convenient way for women to learn how to earn passive income through apartment investing.

Kaylee has completed hundreds of hours of continuing education in real estate. Also, she is constantly learning about multifamily business models to obtain the best return on investment for herself and her partners.

MORE ABOUT KAYLEE

Founder of The Apartment QueenTM

Founder of SheVest APP

Founder of Property ManagementAI

Founder of ReByKaylee LLC Residential Real Estate Brokerage

General partner/Key Principal of a $47.5 MM Assets Under Management Texas, $17.1 MM Assets Under Management Phoenix Arizona

General Partner and Key Principal – Century Tree Apartments

General Partner, Lead Investor, and Key Principal – The Aspens Apartments

General Partner – The Meadows Apartments

General Partner and Key Principal – Village on University Apartments – Denton, TX

General Partner – Los Parados Apartments – Houston, TX

General Partner – The Flats at 2030 – Phoenix, AZ

Lead investor and Key Principal –Leuda May Apartments – Fort Worth, TX

Bachelor's Degree in Molecular and Experimental Nutrition, Texas A&M University

Licensed Real Estate Brokerage owner in the State of Texas

To be considered as one of our SheVestors, take our investor quiz so we can notify you about events and deals. Find "The Apartment Queen™ Investor Questionnaire" at:
https://form.jotform.com/200207883604451

The Apartment Queen

We are looking for more investors like you.

Please complete The Apartment Queen™
Investor Questionnaire to be added to
our list for events and deals:
https://form.jotform.com/200207883604451

Our ideal investor is typically one of these following
Ultimate passive investors:
WOMEN with 1031 Exchange over $400K
High Net Worth Individuals
Doctors
Dentists
Engineers
Individual with 10 Years' Experience at a Company
Real Estate Brokers/Agents
Female Athletes
Aggie Women
Women CEO, Founder
Socialites
Duchess/Heiress
Individuals with Pension Funds
Endowments
Women-owned Family Offices
Those with Funds Who Support the Social Initiative
to Teach Financial Literacy to Women
Angel Investors Supporting Women

CHAPTER 35 – THE APARTMENT QUEEN MANIFESTO

MANIFESTO: BASIC AND BEYOND

The Apartment Queen manifesto captures precisely the embodiment of a true apartment queen. Being part of the community is a complete devotion to helping women attain financial inclusion. Our endeavor is also to identify and develop a plan to end toxic co-dependency and rightfully stand on our own.

AN APARTMENT QUEEN:

- Does not support narcissistic behavior or bullying, including those who bring others down for self-gain or control others through fear.

- Understands the importance of having a team and collaborating with others to achieve common goals. Members of The Apartment Queen community know how to pave the way for other women to invest in real estate.

- Asks as many questions as needed to understand the situation before engaging in an important decision.

- Usually starts questions with "How" or "Why."

- Constantly compliments other queens, is inspired to acquire knowledge and is not envious of others' success.

- Embraces challenges and welcomes transparency even if it uncomfortable.

- Is always available.

- Always has time for self-care and puts her physical and mental health before others.

- Is not afraid to admit mistakes and ask for help.

- Is continuously learning the facets of real estate at all times.

- Asks for help and is willing to help others in any way.

- Does not expect anything in return for her help.

- Listens more than she talks.

- Has solid negotiation skills and is willing to work hard to improve those skills.

- Has an eye for the future, including a five-, ten-, and twenty-year plan.

- Documents these plans and reviews them on a yearly basis or, if possible, quarterly.

- Realizes that the five (5) people with whom she spends the most time are an embodiment of who she will become. She surrounds herself with people who will freely give advice or talk about what they do.

- Considers taking advice only from someone living a successful life with established goals for the future.

- Always asks for what she wants without worrying about how it may make others feel.

- Always wants to lead and excel in a male-dominated industry.

- Establishes her restrictions and makes those clear to those with who she works.

- Offers praise and compliments others on their strengths.

- Is grateful for everything that she has.

- Embodies the character of resiliency.

- Operates with radical open-mindedness, realizing that we do not know the answers to all the questions that may arise.

- Is always true to her word while under-promising and over-delivering.

- Always puts her family first and does not prioritize work over families.

- Operates with solid principles, especially when making difficult decisions.

- Gives credit where credit is due and always celebrates wins, big or small.

- Is transparent and provides feedback regularly to help her team grow.

- Makes decisions with the team in mind and not only for personal gain.

- Always treats others the way she wants to be treated.

- Makes decisions for long-term and short-term strategies.

- Is not intimidated by having the title "Investor" or the status or wealth of other investors.

- Is transparent about what she wants for her business and the entire community.

- Creates equity and net worth for herself and works hard to become an accredited investor.

- Has passive cash flow and will treasure it because of hard-earned principle.

- Shares knowledge to help empower others.

- Surrounds herself with a community of women who are focused on solutions, not problems.

- Talks about ways to improve long-term goals each day.

- Does not gossip.

- Does not complain about misfortune and strives to learn from all experiences to avoid similar situations.

- Pays close attention to what she has without focusing on what she does not have.

- Takes charge of her mental health and regularly speaks with a professional instead of ranting to her family and friends.

- Pays close attention to the tranquility of her mind and will not permit an outside stimulus to ruin her day.

- Knows how to grind but also takes regular vacations.

- Controls her path towards her destiny by being "in-the-loop" and maintaining financial independence.

Chapter 36 – The Apartment Queen Deal Summaries

Village East Apartments Denton Texas

NUMBER OF UNITS	PURCHASE PRICE	PROJECTED RETURNS	TOTAL EQUITY RAISE
133	$12,250,000	19.75%	$4,600,000
Village East is a 133 unit garden-style value add apartment located in Denton, TX, about 30 minutes north of Dallas.	We negotiated a price / door that is $5,000 less than market average in a county that is forecast to experience the strongest economical growth in the U.S. according to Oxford Economics.	Equity partners will receive a preferred return of 7% and projected annualized returns of 19.75%	As sponsors we'll be covering 5% of the equity needed ($230,000) and will partner with accredited investors to syndicate the remaining $4.37M for the project.

Target IRR-16.62 Average

THE ASPENS APARTMENTS (ORIGINALLY LANTANA) 26 UNITS COLORADO CITY, TEXAS

24% Target IRR
Purchased for $675,000

CENTURY TREE APARTMENTS (ORIGINALLY QUAIL RUN) 24 UNITS COLORADO CITY, TEXAS

22.3+% Target IRR
Purchased for $547,000

LOS PRADOS APARTMENTS HOUSTON TEXAS

Los Prados | 125 W Dyna Dr. | Houston, TX
Confidential Investment Summary

THE OPPORTUNITY: AT A GLANCE

9.36%
AVG. ANNUAL DISTRIBUTIONS

86.75%
5-YR TOTAL RETURN

7.0%
REVERSION CAP

15.17%
IRR (PASSIVE)

80/20
LP/GP SPLIT

$75,000
MINIMUM INVESTMENT

THE OPPORTUNITY
AT A GLANCE

$1.2M
TOTAL REHAB

264
UNITS

$23.35M
PURCHASE PRICE

1977
YEAR BUILT

$8.3M
EQUITY RAISE

98%
PHYSCIAL OCCUPANCY

LEUDA MAY APARTMENTS FORT WORTH TEXAS

THE OPPORTUNITY: AT A GLANCE

Flats at 2030 Phoenix AZ

The Flats at 2030 | 2030 W Indian School Rd, Phoenix, AZ
Confidential Investment Summary

The Opportunity: At a Glance

10.15% AVG. ANNUAL DISTRIBUTIONS

104% 5-YR TOTAL RETURN

6.5% REVERSION CAP

17.5% IRR (PASSIVE)

80/20 LP/GP SPLIT

$60,000 MINIMUM INVESTMENT

THE OPPORTUNITY AT A GLANCE

$1.35M TOTAL REHAB

236 UNITS

$16.7M PURCHASE PRICE

1971 YEAR BUILT

$5M EQUITY RATE

98% PHYSCIAL OCCUPANCY

THE MEADOWS DALLAS TEXAS

48 units
IRR 20.21%
Purchase Price 4.7MM

RESOURCES

Chapter 37 – Common Multifamily Investing Terms

Below are some common terms used in our industry.

Accredited Investor

In the United States, to be considered an accredited investor, you must have a net worth of at least $1,000,000, excluding the value of your primary residence, or have an income of at least $200,000 per year for the last two years ($300,000 combined income if married) with the expectation to make the same amount in the future.

Bonus Depreciation

An incentive that allows a business to immediately deduct a large portion if not close to 100%, of its purchase price of eligible assets in the first year of purchase. Established in The Tax Cuts and Jobs Act, it's known as the additional first-year depreciation deduction.

Bridge Loans

Bridge loans bridge the gap between when the Multifamily property owner gets the funds for the property loan and makes any repairs or improvements to the property. Multifamily and commercial real estate bridge loan terms are typically three months to three years. It's best to use a bridge loan when cash is not an option because it requires a far less rigorous analysis for the loan, and the closing period is much shorter.

There's a tradeoff here as interest rates are sometimes double or triple what a conventional loan would be. You can use bridge loans for substantial rehab of a multifamily property and then refinance into conventional Multifamily financing.

BRRRR

(Buy, Rehab, Rent, Refinance, Repeat).
Basis Points
One hundredth of one percent

50 basis points =.50 rate point adjustment

CAPITAL EXPENDITURES (CAPEX) VS. MAINTENANCE?

Capital expenditures are meant to improve the asset's value and are below-the-line expenses in your Profit and Loss statement, meaning capex is deductible from your taxes differently than maintenance costs. It generally is recovered through depreciation; maintenance is a regularly scheduled cost of maintaining the asset in its original condition, such as filters, light bulbs, toilet repairs, etc. We budget maintenance cost as an average per unit, where capex is based on large renovation projects planned for in detail in a business plan.

CAPITALIZATION RATE (CAP RATE)

The Cap Rate is the ratio between net operating income produced by the asset and the original capital cost, also known as the current market value. There is an entry cap rate and an exit cap rate. The entry cap rate is based the asset's current performance (and should closely be related to market average of cap rates) at the time of purchase. The exit cap rate is the adjusted cap rate when you will sell the property. This is often a controversial topic. We always use higher cap rate numbers for the exit cap rate (we assume it is less stabilized at the sale than the purchase, showing asset performance in a recession or major problem when we MUST sell) to account for any performance issues in the economy. It is considered conservative to increase the exit cap rate from entry 75-200 basis points, or less stable than when we bought it. The variance in basis point adjustment at sale depends heavily on current market conditions. But for an area like Dallas/Fort Worth, there is a level of stability and, therefore, less of a cap rate increase on sale. (You can get a higher price regardless).

The formula to calculate the cap rate is as follows:

$$NOI/cap\ rate = market\ value\ or\ sales\ price$$

COMMERCIAL MORTGAGE-BACKED SECURITY (CMBS)

A loan is pooled with other loans then sold to investors for a return, also known as conduit loans. These are long-term, non-recourse loans; however, they come with a hefty prepayment penalty called yield maintenance and defeasance to protect the return expected by the pool of investors.

COST SEGREGATION

In the United States tax laws and accounting rules, cost segregation is the process of removing personal property assets from real property assets. It's used as a strategic tax planning tool that allows companies or individuals who have purchased, rehabbed, remodeled, or expanded any real estate to improve cash flow by accelerating depreciation deductions and deferring state and federal income taxes.

DEBT YIELD

The debt yield is one of the most important risk metrics in multifamily loans. It is the NOI/total loan amount. Lenders use this to determine how long it would take them to recoup their investment if it had to go back to the bank. Many lenders require a minimum debt yield to approve a loan, so it's possible to calculate the maximum loan amount if you know the property's annual income. Lenders want to see a 5 going in, and higher than 8 once stabilized.

GROSS RENT MULTIPLIER (GRM)

GRM is a way to quickly value an asset based on gross rents or determine gross rents based on prices.

$$GRM = Price/Gross\ Rents$$

Think of it as the number of years it would take for gross rents to pay for a property based on today's purchase price.

INTERNAL RATE OF RETURN (IRR)

The IRR considers that the calculation excludes external factors, such as inflation, the cost of money/capital, and other financial risks.

In simple terms, it is the interest rate at which the net present value of all cash flows, including positive and negative, equals zero.

The initial cost of the project is used with estimates of the future cash flows to determine the interest rate.

We use a computer, but you can determine IRR through trial and error by plugging different interest rates into your formulas until you get an NPV close to zero.

A project with a positive Net Present Value (NPV) will also have an IRR that exceeds the cost of capital. AKA thumbs up.

As a rule, businesses should not accept projects with an IRR that exceeds the cost of capital.

INVESTOR SUITABILITY

Investor suitability is a self-certification form that indicates whether the investor is sophisticated, accredited, or neither. Complete this form prior to investment, and before wiring any money. The SEC requires this form.

LOW-INCOME HOUSING TAX CREDITS (LIHTC)

We do not do rent control using this.

PRIVATE PLACEMENT MEMORANDUM (PPM)

This is the Holy Grail of what risks you're about to enter into for an investment. PPM is used across the commercial real estate industry and other industries. Some commercial buildings, developments, apartment investments, and more use this set of documents to show investors what risks could be associated with their investment. You will often see a PPM in groups who are syndicating or pooling money together.

Skin in the Game

The amount of money a sponsor contributes to the deal.

Sophisticated Investors

Based on the U.S. Securities and Exchange Commission (SEC)'s definition, sophisticated investors have enough knowledge and experience in business matters to evaluate the risks and merits of an investment. The SEC exempts small companies from registering certain securities sold to these investors. (Regulation D 506b – we can have up to 35 of these individuals).

Subscription Agreement

The contract investors receive before investing, which is an agreement that the investor has thoroughly read the PPM and understands it, understands what they are purchasing, lists how they would like to receive payment of distributions and profits. They agree to purchase and tinder purchase money with the subscription agreement (wire funds within a specific time frame).

T12 – Trailing Twelve Financials

The *Trailing Twelve Financials* on a property lists all of the income and expenses, as well as the Net Operating Income (NOI).

The Apartment Queen

We are looking for more investors like you.

**Please complete The Apartment Queen™
Investor Questionnaire to be added to
our list for events and deals:**
https://form.jotform.com/200207883604451

Our ideal investor is typically one of these following
Ultimate passive investors:
WOMEN with 1031 Exchange over $400K
High Net Worth Individuals
Doctors
Dentists
Engineers
Individual with 10 Years' Experience at a Company
Real Estate Brokers/Agents
Female Athletes
Aggie Women
Women CEO, Founder
Socialites
Duchess/Heiress
Individuals with Pension Funds
Endowments
Women-owned Family Offices
Those with Funds Who Support the Social Initiative
to Teach Financial Literacy to Women
Angel Investors Supporting Women

Chapter 38 – Recommended Reading

"Women Don't Ask: The High Cost of Avoiding Negotiation—and Positive Strategies for Change" by Sara Laschever and Linda Babcock

"Ask for It! How Women Can Use the Power of Negotiation to Get What They Really Want" by Sara Laschever and Linda Babcock

"The Shadow Negotiation: How Women Can Master the Hidden Agendas That Determine Bargaining Success" by Debra Kolb and Judith Williams

"What Works: Gender Equality by Design" by Iris Bohnet

"What Works for Women at Work: Four Patterns Working Women Need to Know" by Joan C. Williams and Rachel Dempsey

"Never Split the Difference: Negotiating As If Your Life Depended On It" by Chris Voss and Tahl Raz

"Getting to Yes: Negotiating Agreement Without Giving In" by Roger Fisher, William L. Ury, and Bruce Patton

The Apartment Queen

We are looking for more investors like you.

**Please complete The Apartment Queen™
Investor Questionnaire to be added to
our list for events and deals:**
https://form.jotform.com/200207883604451

Our ideal investor is typically one of these following
Ultimate passive investors:
WOMEN with 1031 Exchange over $400K
High Net Worth Individuals
Doctors
Dentists
Engineers
Individual with 10 Years' Experience at a Company
Real Estate Brokers/Agents
Female Athletes
Aggie Women
Women CEO, Founder
Socialites
Duchess/Heiress
Individuals with Pension Funds
Endowments
Women-owned Family Offices
Those with Funds Who Support the Social Initiative
to Teach Financial Literacy to Women
Angel Investors Supporting Women